author United States. Department of Agriculture

Message from the President of the United States

author United States. Department of Agriculture

Message from the President of the United States

ISBN/EAN: 9783742819079

Manufactured in Europe, USA, Canada, Australia, Japa

Cover: Foto ©Andreas Hilbeck / pixelio.de

Manufactured and distributed by brebook publishing software
(www.brebook.com)

author United States. Department of Agriculture

Message from the President of the United States

MESSAGE

FROM THE

PRESIDENT OF THE UNITED STATES,

TRANSMITTING

Documents received from the Commissioner of Agriculture, in reply to resolution of the 7th instant, relative to contagious diseases of cattle.

DECEMBER 13, 1880.—Referred to the Committee on Agriculture and ordered to be printed.

To the Senate of the United States:

The accompanying documents, received from the Commissioner of Agriculture, are transmitted to the Senate, in reply to its resolution of the 7th instant, relating to the contagions diseases of cattle.

R. B. HAYES.

EXECUTIVE MANSION, *December* 13, 1880.

DEPARTMENT OF AGRICULTURE,
Washington, D. C., December 9, 1880.

To the PRESIDENT:

I have the honor to submit herewith certain papers covering the information required by the Senate under the resolution offered December the 7th, instant, by the Hon. John W. Johnston, Senator from Virginia.

First. The order directing Dr. Charles P. Lyman, F. R. C. V. S., to proceed to England for the purposes therein set forth.

Second. Dr. Lyman's report of the work performed in pursuance of this order, and of other investigations relative to contagions diseases of cattle that were required of him.

I have also the honor to submit, as appendices to this information, "An extract from the annual report of the Veterinary Department of the Privy Council Office of Great Britain, 1879;" the opinion of Prof. W. Williams, a pathological author of renown, that the disease landed in England prior to the embargo, and supposed by the privy council to be pleuro-pneumonia, was not so in fact; and a copy of "The contagious diseases (animals) act and orders for Great Britain."

Very respectfully, your obedient servant,

WM. G. LE DUC,
Commissioner of Agriculture.

DEPARTMENT OF AGRICULTURE,
Washington, D. C., June 14, 1880.

SIR: You are hereby directed to proceed to Great Britain at your early convenience, and there to continue your investigation into pleuro-pneumonia as affecting American cattle, and into any matters that may be connected with their exportation and the improvement of the trade in these animals between that country and our own.

You will keep a correct account of all expenses and make report to this department of your progress as often as possible during your absence.

Very respectfully,

WM. G. LE DUC,
Commissioner of Agriculture.

Dr. CHARLES P. LYMAN,
Springfield, Mass.

CONTAGIOUS PLEURO-PNEUMONIA.

REPORT OF CHARLES P. LYMAN, F. R. C. V. S.

Sir: In my last report to you upon contagious pleuro-pneumonia, I pointed out, as thoroughly as any means for investigation which I then had would enable me to do, the States and counties wherein animals affected with this disease could be found. It was thought at that time, and no investigation since then has been able to show differently, that these counties, or those lying very close to them, contained all the cases that could be found in the United States. Supposing I had succeeded in thus mapping out the whole of our infected district, I began pushing inquiries in a new direction, and for this purpose the following letter was written to one of the most prominent veterinary surgeons and authors in England:

SPRINGFIELD, MASS., *May* 10, 1880.

DEAR SIR: I mail you herewith a copy of my report to the Commissioner of Agriculture on pleuro-pneumonia contagiosa. From it you will be able to see *exactly* to what extent we are infected. The facts to which I especially call your attention are these:

1st. That our ports of Portland, in the State of Maine, and Boston, in the State of Massachusetts, are not in or anywhere near the infected districts; no nearer in fact, I believe, than are some of the free continental ports or provinces to some of the infected ones.

2d. That the cattle coming to those ports for shipment, and indeed for all uses, come entirely from the West—one, two, and even more thousands of miles away from our infected districts.

3d. That the lines of rail over which these cattle are carried going to these ports do not pass through or go anywhere near the infected districts.

4th. That our Western States are free, luckily for us, and always have been, of this scourge.

Now, under these circumstances, is there any method which suggests itself to you by which the Government of Great Britain can be induced to raise the embargo against our cattle coming to her from these free districts, and through these free ports? If you think there is any chance for the matter being arranged the Commissioner of Agriculture will, I think, be very glad to enter into negotiations upon the subject.

Very truly,

C. P. LYMAN.

GEORGE FLEMING, F. R. C. V. S.,
Veterinary Surgeon, Second Life Guards, London, England.

To which, in due time, the following answer was received:

LONDON, *June* 24, 1880.

Dr. CHARLES P. LYMAN:

Please excuse my delay in replying to your two letters. I have been away on a tour of army inspection, and only returned yesterday. Very many thanks for your report on contagious pleuro-pneumonia. I very much fear there is not the slightest chance of the embargo on American cattle being raised in this country until the States are entirely free from the malady, notwithstanding the fact you point out that there is an immense extent of country uninfected. So long as only one State, or one portion of a State, is contaminated, so long, depend upon it, will the present law continue. Even the present government, which when not in office strenuously opposed the law, brought into office with regard to United States cattle, is now most determined to carry it out. If it were relaxed in the case of the United States it would have to be

3

so also in the case of Russia and Germany, with respect to cattle plague, and then this country would certainly not be safe. Commerce spreads these diseases. The feeling here is to keep this country free from infectious animal diseases, after we have stamped them out at an awful cost and trouble; and to allow live stock to enter from anywhere where these diseases exist would not be heard of. Whenever the United States is certified to be a clean country, the embargo will be raised. Your government is not taking active steps to free the States from pleuro-pneumonia, and there is no knowing how far it may spread. So long as the government is indifferent to this matter, so long will your people suffer from the embargo. The losses from contagious diseases here have been so terrible, through a similar apathy, that the authorities are now fully aroused.

With regard to the transit of American cattle, I cannot say anything which would be of much value to you; but I would recommend you to write to Professor Brown, veterinary department, privy council office, London. He knows everything pertaining to the shipment and carriage of cattle, and will, I have no doubt, afford you every information.

As for myself, I shall only be too glad to assist you all I can, and in offering to do so I take once more the opportunity of renewing a paper friendship, which I trust will be converted into something more substantial should you visit England.

Believe me to be, yours, very truly,

GEORGE FLEMING.

Before this answer was received, however, the department was in receipt of the report of the Veterinary Department of the Privy Council of Great Britain for 1879 (see appendix), when, as you will remember, I addressed to you the following communication:

WASHINGTON, D. C., *June* 12, 1880.

SIR: In the report of the veterinary department of the privy council of Great Britain for the year 1879, which report has just been received, on page 7 appears the following: "The most notable event of the past year in connection with the trade in foreign animals was the removal of the United States of America from the list of countries from which cattle could be imported as healthy, owing to the landing at different times during the year of animals affected with pleuro-pneumonia." The first known such importation is said to have been made from the steamship Dominion from Portland, Me., about January 14. Next, the detection of the same disease in the cargo of the Ontario afforded further evidence of its existence among cattle in the United States. "Cargoes of cattle, among which pleuro-pneumonia was detected, continued to arrive," until finally an order was passed (February 10) the effect of which was to cause the slaughter of all cattle from the States at the place of landing in Great Britain. It is perhaps worth noticing in passing that Prof. W. Williams, of Edinburgh, one of those called upon by the authorities to examine the Ontario lungs, says: "Since first arrival of Ontario with cattle others have arrived at Liverpool, and I have examined the lungs said by privy council inspectors to have pleuro-pneumonia, and satisfied all who have seen them that no pleuro-pneumonia has arrived here from America; indeed, every one is surprised that such a gross mistake should have been made." (Same report, p. 9.)

As you will remember, my recent investigation into this matter shows that our ports of Baltimore, Philadelphia, Jersey City, and New York are the only ones that are in our infected districts. In this report of the privy council the only ports referred to by name as having sent diseased cattle are Portland and Boston. This is most strange, and if true means that we have pleuro-pneumonia among our western herds, as the animals shipped from the two ports come in every case from the West, not passing through or anywhere near the district which we know is infected.

During my recent investigation every means at command was used to ascertain if this disease had an existence among our western herds. Every inquiry possible was made, and hundreds of lungs from slaughtered animals coming from all parts of the West were examined, and the result seemed to show that there was not, nor never had been, any pleuro-pneumonia in that part of our country.

Here, then, are two seeming facts which are in direct antagonism. The English examinations show, beyond doubt, that our western cattle, upon being landed there, exhibit unmistakable signs that pleuro-pneumonia exists among them. My own investigation on the other hand, conducted with the greatest thoroughness, shows that pleuro-pneumonia does not exist West.

And now, as the determination of this question, one way or the other, is a matter of great importance to the immense cattle interests of our country, it would seem to be right that the investigation already commenced should be carried to the other side, and an American inspection be made of the cattle coming into Liverpool; then, having found there a few of these numerously reported cases, to trace them back by means of the way-bills, &c., over their course of travel, to their original starting point in the West, or as near to it as possible.

Very respectfully,

CHARLES P. LYMAN.

Hon. WILLIAM G. LE DUC,
Commissioner of Agriculture.

The result of this communication was that, at your direction, on the 23d of June last, I left New York for Liverpool, and arrived there on the 4th day of July; proceeded at once to Edinburgh, Scotland, and called upon Prof. W. Williams, F. R. S. E., and principal of the new veterinary college; who, you will remember, was one of the three experts originally selected to examine the diseased lungs taken from the American cattle which had been landed from the Ontario on January 26, 1879, and the only one of them who positively declared in public that the affection was not contagious pleuro-pneumonia. Professor Williams stated that during the six months succeeding the arrival of the Ontario he had examined portions of the lungs of fully three-fourths of all the animals that had been found diseased, and that he has still not the slightest hesitation in saying that in no case has he found them to exhibit the characteristic lesions of contagious pleuro-pneumonia. He said that Mr. Welsby, a veterinary surgeon living in Derby, near Liverpool, was employed by the steamer people, Messrs Warren & Co., to examine these animals, in company with Mr. Moore, veterinary surgeon to the privy council and inspector of the port of Liverpool, whose procedure was, as soon as an affected lung was found to make a section of the most diseased portion which was sent up to London for the inspection of the chief of his department. Mr. Welsby would at the same time secure a similar piece and send to Professor Williams; therefore he believed that he had an equal chance with the London authorities for a good examination. He also made several trips to Liverpool and examined the beasts and their lungs while they were being slaughtered. The correspondence with Mr. Welsby was then shown me. · A letter of March 16, 1879, accompanied portions of lungs from three different animals, which were condemned by the port inspector as showing the lesions of pleuro-pneumonia contagiosa. These pieces were shown to me and presented simply the lesions of bronchitis with collapse. In a letter of March 17, he writes:

WEST DERBY, *Liverpool, England.*

DEAR MR. WILLIAMS: By the time you receive this the portions of lung I am forwarding will have come to your hand, and which I fear you will declare true cases. Each piece is from a separate animal, and these have arrived per the Ontario, the vessel that brought the cattle you were in Liverpool about a short time since. In examining fifty-five lungs to-day twelve were found similarly affected (some a little more) to the specimens sent you. I should be glad if you will wire me by 10:30 a. m. to-morrow * * * what your opinion is * * *

In haste, yours faithfully,

J. WELSBY.

These portions of lungs were shown me, and exhibited, as did the others, simply the lesions of bronchitis with collapse. On March 18, he writes: " I have not agreed with the opinion expressed here about any of them, but am doubtful about a piece of the last lot sent you. In London they have *no doubt.*" On March 24: " With regard to the animals when living, I had opportunities of seeing them daily; they appeared well; no cough; breathing and temperature normal, and eating well." On April 21: " No more specimens are wanted in *London.*" On May 19: " Have sent to Professor Walley also specimens from cattle received by steamship Minnesota; he agrees with us in this, but says that it was zymotic pleuro-pneumonia on Ontario." On June 7 he writes: "I am commencing to direct attention to the Canadian cattle instead of Western States. Mr. Moore sent a piece of lung from a Canadian ox to London on Thursday, and informed me it was typical of contagious pleuro-pneumonia, and expected Professor Duguid down, but instead, a telegram came, ordering their release if no further disease was found; two others were then slaughtered, and I was requested to be present; they were perfectly healthy. I was sorry that I could not send you a piece of the lung that went to London, but no doubt shall have an opportunity of doing so before long." Here I was given a piece of lung which certainly showed lesions resembling those of contagious pleuro-pneumonia more than did any other specimen that I saw in the Professor's possession; it was said to be from the Canadian case above referred to, but had been in spirits so long that a satisfactory examination could not be made. Professor Williams, however, declared that in his opinion even it was not the disease, but that it looked more like it than did anything else he had seen from our side of the water.

In the new edition of his book on Veterinary Medicine Professor Williams has gone into the matter thoroughly, not only in the text, but by colored lithographic plates, which are said by all who saw the pieces of lung which were sent to Edinburgh to be remarkably like them. In the appendix the whole of this matter will be found reproduced.

I next saw Professor Walley, principal of the Edinburgh Veterinary College, who holds an appointment in Edinburgh under the Veterinary Privy Council, and was one of those who went to Liverpool and examined as an expert the lungs from some of the Ontario cattle. He said: "I was called to Liverpool, and there shown animals together in a building, which I was told came per steamship Ontario from America; a few of them were coughing, I should judge giving the pathognomonic cough of contagious pleuro-pneumonia. I examined them; they gave no elevation of temperature that amounted to anything as a sign; they varied a little; some would be a degree higher than others, but nothing remarkable in any. While this examination was going on, and before we had finished to my entire satisfaction, a man came to say that we were wanted in the slaughter-house, where we went at once, and found two animals, that we were told had been taken hap-hazard from this cargo of the Ontario, hanging partially dressed, and from these I saw lungs taken that exhibited to me, without any doubt, the well-known lesions of contagious pleuro-pneumonia. I was not at the place for more than an hour and Professor McCall, principal of the Glasgow Veterinary College, was the only veterinarian with me. Mr. Hall, the consignee, or his agent, was there, and said that there was no doubt about this; "that it really was pleuro." In answer to questions the Professor said the animals were in as good a condition as any of the others—i. e., about half fat; that there were several diseased spots in their lungs, and that the largest was about the size of the crown of a Derby hat; that the diseased portions were "marbled," and the parenchyma varied in color from deep red to pink, but it was mostly of a pinkish shade; that there was no attempt towards the formation of a cyst-wall around any of the diseased portions, because the disease had not been of sufficient standing.

Being asked if he did not think it strange that contagious pleuropneumonia should exist to so great an extent and the animal be as fat as any of the rest, and still have no elevation of temperature, and no encysted portion of lungs, he answered that he had had no opportunity of examining these animals before death as to temperature or anything else, and could give no idea as to how they looked when alive. He regretted that no one had saved a piece of these lungs—it ought to have been done. Since that, which was the only time he had been in Liverpool on this business, he had examined several *pieces* of lungs said to be from American cattle, and they had *not* exhibited to him lesions of contagious pleuro-pneumonia, but of broncho-pneumonia, and the colored plate in Professor Williams's book was a fairly good representation of their appearance, but it did not represent *at all* the appearance of the lungs that he had examined in Liverpool said to be from the Ontario cargo. He was told that these two cattle that he saw in the Liverpool slaughter-house had been drafted at random from the cargo of the Ontario by Mr. Hall.

From Edinburg I proceeded to London and the office of the veterinary department of the Privy Council. In the absence of Professor Brown, the chief of the department, I saw Mr. Cope, the chief inspector, who kindly showed me what specimens they had of "American pleuro." They were few in number and very small in size, and had been in preservative fluid so long that they were very much altered. They were very different from those I had been shown in Edinburg—said to be the same—(see p. 5, Mr. Wellsby's proceedings) having very much more the appearance of the contagious pleuro-pneumonia, of which the former showed *nothing.* "Animals affected with pleuro-pneumonia," said Mr. Cope, "come to us from the ports of Baltimore, Philadelphia, New York, Boston, and Portland, and we are now (July 12) receiving more than ever of it. You can see it for yourself by going either to Deptford or Liverpool, but Liverpool would be the best place." I was informed by this gentleman that formerly the Privy Council had power to release from the restriction a part of any country that they saw fit; but now it must be a whole country, if any, and that could not be until the whole of that country was absolutely free from disease. Anything else would need the action of Parliament. There is absolutely no option in the matter—the rule or law must govern. (See appendix.) In answer to a question Mr. Cope said that they had never had a suspicion of Canadian cattle. (See p. 6.) Subsequently I was fortunate enough to see Professor Brown, veterinarian-in-chief to the department.

I asked him, supposing drafts of cattle were made from our healthy western districts, transported over lines of rail which were entirely away from our infected districts, in cars used for these and no other cattle, if inspectors could guarantee that they had not been in the same yard, or mixed with any other cattle on the route or at the port of embarkation, and were healthy at time of shipment, and inspection at the port of debarkation should show that cargo after cargo coming under these regulations could be landed free from pleuro-pneumonia, would the embargo be raised in favor of cattle so inspected from such a port? To this Professor Brown answered that even if England were disposed to remove the restriction from any one port under certain methods of inspection, as he understood it, the United States were not, as matters now stood, able to prevent cattle coming to said port from any point that people chose to send them. I told him that I thought the matter could undoubtedly be arranged with the State authorities and railroad companies so as to be perfectly safe. He intimated that this would be too loose an arrangement to give England much confidence, and further said that he did not know what there was to prevent a diseased or infected animal from being sent at any time from the infected eastern district directly to the parts in the west from which these drafts were being made. The Government of the United States, as a government, had not as yet shown the slightest interest in the matter, and that, in the absence of any national laws relating to the movements of animals exposed to or infected with contagious diseases, he should not advise any change from their present methods. Here a representation was made setting forth the sovereignty of States and their powers—that a State could make any laws upon the subject that she thought proper, providing it did not conflict with the Constitution of the United States. In answer to this the opinion given was that decidedly, in this matter, these could not take the place of national laws; that it would be highly impracticable for Great Britain to recognize independent State governments while dealing with the United States.

Following is a list, which was kindly furnished me by the veterinary department, giving the cargoes of cattle among which pleuro-pneumonia had been detected, and which had arrived from our ports of Boston and Portland (thought to be free from disease) since January 1, 1880.

Date.	Steamer.	From—	To—	Number of cases of pleuro-pneumonia.
Jan. 11	Milanesian	Boston	London	*12
16	Massachusetts	do	Liverpool	9
Feb. 4	Palestino	do	do	2
7	Bavarian	do	do	3
10	Lake Nepigon	Portland	do	2
12	Brazilian	Boston	do	10
12	Iowa	do	do	16
17	Canopus	do	do	1
20	Salerno	do	Hull	2
21	Bulgarian	do	Liverpool	3
26	Lake Winnipeg	Portland	do	1
27	Bohemian	Boston	do	3
March 4	Massachusetts	do	do	7
4	Illyrian	do	do	7
20	Palestine	do	do	3
24	Iowa	do	do	4
27	Egypt	do. (?)	do	1
30	Glamorgan	do	do	3
April 18	Massachusetts	do	do	5
30	Iberian	do	do	1
May 5	Lake Nepigon	Portland	London	1
19	Bohemian	Boston	Liverpool	4
20	Illyrian	do	do	13
June 2	Victoria	do	do	4

* Two died.

At Deptford, which is the foreign animals' wharf for London, I at this time saw some twenty-seven hundred head of American bullocks tied up waiting slaughter; they had been received mostly from New York, a few from Baltimore. From the ocean steamers these beasts are landed some distance down the river, and from there reshipped in a transport which brings them directly to the landing-stages for this wharf. This transport boat is thoroughly disinfected after each cargo.

From London I proceeded to Liverpool, arriving there on the 13th of July. Cattle from the United States arriving in this port are allowed to land at three different places, namely, the Huskisson Branch Docks No. 2, on the Liverpool side of the river, at Woodside and Wallasey landing-stages on the Birkenhead side, and at these places only. For their reception, and the accommodation of the trade, under the present restrictions, the dock company have fitted up on the wharves fine buildings to serve as stables for the cattle while alive, also slaughter-houses and cooling rooms.

The law allows the animal to remain alive not longer than fourteen

days after debarkation, during which time he must remain in this build
ing, subject to a certain daily charge, payable to the dock company.
After each cargo has been disposed of, the whole of the premises are
most thoroughly cleaned before being again filled, and if any such contagious malady as foot-and-mouth disease has been found they are thoroughly disinfected, and if thought necessary all the manure and other
litter with which they may have been in contact is destroyed, under the
direction of the Veterinary Department, but at the expense of the dock
company.

With the credentials furnished me from the Privy Council office I called
upon the Veterinary Inspector of the port, Mr. J. W. T. Moore, F. R. C. V. S.,
and requested to be allowed to accompany him for a time in his daily inspections. To this he kindly assented, and during the whole of my stay
showed me every attention and rendered me every assistance within his
power. His method of inspection is to make an examination of the live animals within as nearly as possible twelve hours after the landing of a cargo.
For this purpose the beasts are driven into the stables and tied up facing a
passage way. Down this the inspector passes, noticing carefully each beast.
If anything unusual is observed in any one case, the animal is made the
subject of a minute examination, when, if found particularly diseased, he
is either put by himself or slaughtered at once. This examination being
completed and the cargo "passed," the owners are at liberty to commence slaughtering as soon as they wish. In the slaughter-house the
men have orders not to allow any lung or *portion* of it to be taken away
until it has been inspected by Mr. Moore. For the purposes of this lung
inspection this product of the whole day's killing is hung up, and once
each day every slaughter-house where killing is going on is visited by
the inspector, and every lung carefully examined by him. If any one is
found which he considers exhibits the lesions of pleuro-pneumonia it is
destroyed, and an inquiry made which soon shows beyond a doubt exactly to what cargo the affected animal belonged.

On July 14, 210 bullocks, the cargo of the steamship Carolina from
Baltimore, were examined, and four of these were condemned by the inspector as being "suspicious" of pleuro-pneumonia. However, upon
post-mortem examination nothing of the sort was found.

On July 15, the steamship Federico, from Norfolk, Virginia, landed
128 bullocks and a carcass. A *post-mortem* examination of this carcass
showed that the animal had been trampled to death; seven of the ribs
were broken. During the lung examination to-day two pairs were found
that were condemned as showing the lesions of pleuro-pneumonia. One
pair showed plainly and plentifully the peculiar lesions of tuberculosis,
and in addition contained several small spots in which the changes supposed to be peculiar to pleuro-pneumonia could be plainly seen, and upon
which they were condemned. The history of these animals, so far as it
could be procured in Liverpool, was, that Mr. Smith bought of Mr. Rod-
dick 194 bullocks *ex* steamship Brazilian from Boston, July 7. These
were consigned to the seller by J. &. C. Coughlin, of London, Canada,
but were from the United States; there were two hundred of them; five
died on the passage. The inspector here saw the lungs of some of these
that were landed dead, and found death to have occurred from causes
other than pleuro-pneumonia.

July 16.—A case of pleuro-pneumonia was reported by Mr. Moore as
coming on the Iberian from Boston, but the lung lesion was so very small
(scarcely as large as a filbert) and its appearance was such that it seemed
to me very doubtful if even the semblance of the disease was present.

July 17.—Examined *ex* steamship Malta, from Boston, 397 bullocks.

Five were landed dead, and one was killed on landing. One of the five landed dead was so much decomposed as to prevent a satisfactory examination. The lungs of the other four were emphysematous only.

July 19.—Two lungs from beasts which came on the steamship Victoria, from Boston, were reported as showing pleuro-pneumonia, the largest "spot" being about 1¼ inches in its largest diameter, and situated exactly at the root of the lung, indurated to the touch, and upon being cut into exhibited the usual "marbled" appearance of pleuro-pneumonia, but in the center of the "spot" appeared a small, rounded body not larger than one-fourth inch in diameter, the exact nature of which future microscopic examination will probably determine. This was surrounded by a layer scarcely a line wide of what seemed to the naked eye to be a thin pus of a grayish color; this, in its turn, by a thin membranous wall; this, again, by the "marbled" appearance already referred to, the interlobular effusion and thickening being well marked. The lungs of one of these beasts had one, the other three, of these "spots." These animals were sent by Timothy Coughlin, London, Canada, but were animals from the United States.

July 20.—At Canada docks were examined 222 cattle, *ex* steamship Texas, from Montreal. One of these animals, a fat cow, was breathing rapidly and had a temperature of 104° F. She was killed and the lungs examined, but no indication of pleuro-pneumonia was found. Inspector Moore assured me that he had repeatedly had this done, always with the same result.

July 23.—To-day was found a good specimen of what the port inspector regards as showing the lesions of pleuro-pneumonia in the lung of a beast from the cargo of the Aleppo, from New York. These animals were shipped by Charles Kalm, of New York, and by their look did not seem to be "westerners."

I have thought best to make these few extracts from my diary, as they refer to all the cases that were condemned during my stay, and also as they help to show the manner in which the work is done. I have also prepared a table which will show the number of animals landed in Liverpool from the United States from the 2d of July to the 13th of August, most of which I had the privilege of examining alive and dead during my stay. You will observe that the percentage reported by Mr. Moore as affected with pleuro-pneumonia is very small indeed, there being only six such out of 10,670 animals examined.

The animals coming from Canada are landed at wharves entirely separate from those used for the trade with the United States. The animals coming off ship-board are tied up in houses furnished for the purpose, and after a twelve hours' rest and quarantine are subjected to a not very close inspection by the veterinary officer of the port, when, if no contagious disease is found—and there never has been as yet—they are allowed to go inland on the hoof without any further restriction. In this way they become scattered to such an extent before being slaughtered that it was impossible for me to see the lungs as I did those of our own cattle; and, indeed, no officer gives them *any* examination except in so far as has already been stated.

Table showing number of animals landed in Liverpool from the United States, from June 2 to August 13.

Steamship	From port of—	Date landed.	Cattle.	Sheep.	Hogs.	Remarks.
Olympus	Boston	July 2	391			
Saint Albans	New York	July 9	392	239		
Palmyra	do	July 13	296	288		
Bulgarian	Boston	July 7	434		222	
Carolina	Baltimore	July 13	210			
Iberian	Boston	July 14	434			1 case condemned as pleuro-pneumonia; 6 very small centers of disease.
Brazilian	do	July 7	569	1,314		2 cases condemned as pleuro-pneumonia: centers very small.
Federico	Norfolk	July 14	129			
Victoria	Boston	July 15	597			2 cases condemned as pleuro-pneumonia; very small centers.
Cella	New York	July 15	98	306	375	
Malta	Boston	July 16	398			
Aleppo	New York	July 18	282	719		1 case condemned as pleuro-pneumonia, and by far the best lesion found.
Massachusetts	Boston	July 19	519	230	483	11 cases swine fever.
Minnesota	do	July 21	416	860		
Palestine	do	July 26	366	815		
Bavarian	do	July 25	441			
Pembroke	do	July 28	294	561	287	7 cases swine fever.
Bohemian	do	July 30	435			3 cases foot-and-mouth disease in cattle.
Tuscany	Philadelphia	July 30	224			
Illyrian	Boston	Aug. 1	437			
Istrian	do	Aug. 5	438			
Iowa	do	Aug. 5	805		207	13 cases resembling splenic apoplexy; 5 cases swine fever.
Enrique	Norfolk	Aug. 6	122			
Gracia	Baltimore	Aug. 8	130			
Canopus	Boston	Aug. 9	444			
Bulgarian	do	Aug. 10	427			
Brazilian	do	Aug. 13	660	618	363	10 cases sheep-scab.
Sicily	Philadelphia	Aug. 13	282			

Total number of animals landed:

Cattle 10,670
Sheep 5,960
Hogs 2,237
Number condemned as having pleuro-pneumonia .... cattle.. 6
Number condemned as having foot-and-mouth disease .... do... 3
Number condemned as having scab .... sheep.. 10
Number condemned as having swine fever .... hogs.. 23

RÉSUMÉ.

About February 1, 1880, the Department of Agriculture, under the act providing for an inquiry into the contagious diseases of domesticated animals, commenced an investigation, the result of which should declare, if possible, the *exact* extent of territory in which there existed any cattle affected with contagious pleuro-pneumonia, on account of which the Government of Great Britain had placed a restriction upon all cattle coming from the United States.

After due time and a thoroughly-conducted investigation, this territory was defined to be one extending (at that time) from Fairfield County, in Connecticut, over New York City and portions of the State of New York lying just north of it; Brooklyn, Long Island, and parts of the island lying just east of it; Jersey City, and over a considerable portion of the State of New Jersey; Philadelphia, and some of the more south-easterly counties of Pennsylvania to Baltimore, and over portions of the more northeasterly counties of Maryland. Further than this, in any locality it was impossible to find a case of the disease, although efforts were made in all directions, and especially among the cattle coming from the same parts of the West as did most of the cattle going to Europe.

Reports were constantly being received, however, from England that cattle affected with pleuro-pneumonia were being frequently landed there. A very short investigation on this side demonstrated clearly that these animals came directly, in nearly all cases, from the West, and oftentimes over lines of rail that were entirely away from any point at which the disease could be located. The next step, therefore, seemed to be to carry the investigation to the other side, to see the diseased cattle as landed there, and, by means of manifests, way-bills, &c., to trace them back to their original starting points in the West, and thus establish the object of the investigation, namely, to find *all* the infected territory.

This was done, and out of nearly eleven thousand beasts landed and examined in Liverpool during parts of July and August, in no one of which could pleuro-pneumonia be detected in the *living* animal, the inspector of the Veterinary Department of the Privy Council condemned, after *post-mortem* examination of the lungs, six cases. These six cases have been traced back, and in all except one it has been found that the animals undoubtedly came from the West, and over lines of rail which are entirely north of any localities that are known to be contaminated, the fact being that a part of their journey eastward was generally made through portions of Canada. This of course means that we have this dreaded cattle scourge established among our Western herds ; that Chicago, Buffalo, Albany, Boston, or Portland are diseased centers, or else the disease is not pleuro-pneumonia at all.

If pleuro-pneumonia exists in the West, or there are diseased centers in or about the points named through which the cattle pass on their journey eastward, the information now in possession of this department will insure its exact location after a little further time for examination.

In relation to the last phase of the matter, all that can at present be said is, that the particular lungs exhibited present, *in their fresh state* and to the naked eye, ALL the lesions of the contagious disease, but on a VERY SMALL SCALE, and in addition there is another lesion that is *constantly* present in these condemned lungs which has never been described by any authority or noticed by any of our veterinarians to be a constant or even a known accompaniment of the disease in question. What bearing this fact may have upon this part of the question a further and more minute investigation of the subject alone can decide. Professor William Williams, of Edinburgh, a comparative pathologist of world-wide celebrity, asserts that the lungs examined by him previous to my visit did not show the lesions of the disease, but that the changes noticed were caused by bronchitis.*

Whether these cases are or are not due to true contagious pleuro-pneumonia is a matter which does not in the mean time have much bearing upon the question of the removal of the English embargo upon our cattle. While we have pleuro-pneumonia in *any* part of our country, and certainly while we have no national legislation looking in any way towards restricting its spread, and its eventual total suppression, just so long the embargo must and will continue to operate against one of our best commercial interests, and to lay that portion of our agriculturists in the West who are engaged in the raising and feeding of fine beef

---

* See Appendix. Also conversation with Professor Williams, page 5 of this report.

bullocks under a very severe and unmerited tax, one which, in the estimation of a very good judge of the matter, has reached, during the present year, a sum rising $2,250,000.* What are the actual losses sustained from the presence of the disease, by the farmers and dairymen of the East who are unfortunate enough to be located in the midst of a contaminated center, it is very hard to say; but that the annual losses by death alone can be no very light tax to them is a safe conclusion.

Then, again, while it is still possible to exterminate this ruinous foreign plague, because it is, we most certainly believe, confined to animals that are kept upon fenced farms, should it *once*, by any misfortune, be carried among the great herds that breed, grow, and feed upon the unfenced ranges of the West, its extirpation would become IMPOSSIBLE. The whole Western country, from Texas northward, would become infected; notwithstanding all efforts that *then* might be made to remedy the evil, this great and growing national interest would be perpetually mortgaged, and there would be an almost incalculable annual loss from deaths alone.

The one remedy *now* for all of this is plain, and of comparatively easy accomplishment, viz: Let Congress enact such measures, and authorize such an execution of them, as shall immediately restrict the movements of cattle out from and within infected districts, and in time eradicate every case of lung plague.

SOUTHERN CATTLE FEVER.

This disease,† widely known as "the Texas cattle fever," although it has never as yet reached Great Britain, and, therefore, has never been put upon the schedule as one of the contagious diseases coming from the United States, and requiring restriction, is one that, for a short time in each year, causes such immense losses among the animals belonging to Western, Northern, and Eastern cattle-growers, dealers, and shippers, that its mention in connection with this report seems to be quite in place.

Beginning, generally, towards the last of July, and extending, with increasing destructiveness, until the time of frost, Western and Northern cattle that have been in contact, in certain ways, with some of the cattle coming from several of the more southerly portions of the country (these seeming perhaps to be in perfect health), contract this fever, which, to them, is much more fatal than it seems to be among the Southern animals, often killing a proportion as high as 90 per cent. of those affected.

A very curious, but still undoubtedly true, feature of the malady is, that these sick Northern animals are not able in any way to communicate the disease to other animals. Its incubation may be from fifteen to forty days. During this period the beast may be shipped from the West, and slaughtered in the East for human food;‡ or it may be placed on board ship and started for the English market, where it is destined seldom, if ever, to arrive, for dying in mid-ocean its carcass is thrown

---

* See Special Report No. 22, page 179, Department of Agriculture, for argument in favor of national legislation.
† See report of Dr. D. E. Salmon, page 98, Special Report No. 22, Department of Agriculture.
‡ In 1868, the Metropolitan Board of Health found that the use of meat from animals affected with Southern fever caused an enormous increase in the death-rate by diarrheal diseases, and especially was there developed an utterly obstinate and incurable class of choleric diarrheas.—(Dr. D. E. Salmon, Special Report No. 22, Department of Agriculture, page 117.)

overboard and becomes a total loss to the owner or those insuring its safe arrival.*

Heavy losses from this cause are also sustained each season by the farmers and dealers in all parts of the North, West, and East; but perhaps the greatest sufferers of all are the breeders and growers of cattle who are so unfortunate as to be located in the States through which the Texans pass on their journey to market, and the States suffering more particularly in this way this past season have undoubtedly been Missouri † and Illinois, although nearly every other State into which the Texans were shipped, from Kansas to Massachusetts, have suffered to a greater or less extent.

How these losses in connection with the foreign trade occur and how they are divided up can readily be seen from the following : ‡

In June 10,642 animals were shipped to Liverpool; 114 died—loss about 1 per cent.

In July 12,137 animals were shipped to Liverpool ; 110 died—loss less than 1 per cent.

In August 9,464 animals were shipped to Liverpool ; 272 died—loss over 2 per cent.

In September 10,826 animals were shipped to Liverpool ; 619 died—loss over 5 per cent.

This shows a loss in September over June of, say, $67,662.50, which excess of loss is considered by the insurance people to be due entirely to Texas fever, and to verify this we have the following quotations of the rates of insurance :

In August, 1880, the Canadian and English companies charged 2¼ to 2½ per cent. from Montreal. At the same time the rates on American cattle from Boston were from 3 to 6 per cent., the highest rates obtaining against Missouri and Illinois beasts.

During September the Canadian and English rates were 2¾ to 3 per cent. from Montreal. The rates on American cattle during the first half of this same month were 5 to 7 per cent.; during the second half, from

---

* For additional particulars relating to this fever, see report of Professor Gamgee to the Commissioner of Agriculture, on the diseases of cattle in the United States, 1871 ; Report of the New York State Cattle Commissioners for 1868, made in connection with the Report of the Metropolitan Board of Health, in relation to the Texas cattle disease, 1869 ; also, the proceedings and debates of the American Convention of Cattle Commissioners, held at Springfield, Ill., December 1, 2, and 3, 1868. Published at Springfield (Ill.), Journal Printing Office, 1869.

† As tending to show what the feeling among these farmers has been, I copy the following from Professor Gamgee's Report, page 82. It is an extract from a letter of Mr. S. Morgan Welsh, contained in the Prairie Farmer of 26th September, 1868 : "Talk," he writes, " to a Missourian about moderation when a drove of Texas cattle is coming, and he will call you a fool, while he coolly loads his gun and joins his neighbors ; and they in end no scare either. They mean to kill, do kill, and will keep killing until the drove takes the back track ; and the drovers must be careful not to get between their cattle and the citizens, either, unless they are bullet-proof. No doubt this looks a good deal like border-ruffianism to you, but it is the way we keep clear of the Texas fever, and, my word for it, Illinois will have to do the same thing yet. Congress ought to do s mething in regard to this stock."

In this same connection, but on the other side, I may say that I recently met a gentleman who says that with two others he went South and bought a large drove of Texans and started North with them. They got along very well until a certain point was reached, when they were met by these self-appointed officers of " the shot-gun quarantine," and obliged to turn back, and they were repeatedly obliged to go back and around until most of their cattle had died and their resources used up, when they came North alone, losers of every cent they had invested in the enterprise, which, in the case of my informant, was all that he had in the world.

‡ I have only had opportunity as yet to personally investigate this one branch of the subject, and that even imperfectly and, as it were, unsystematically, while carrying on the work on contagious pleuro-pneumonia. ⁄

$5\frac{1}{2}$ to 10 per cent.; that is, Ohio cattle could be insured at from 5 to $6\frac{1}{2}$ per cent., Missouri from $6\frac{1}{2}$ to 10 per cent. These differences in insurance make a total on a cargo of, say, 300 beasts, of $2,635 against Missouri, $1,312 against Ohio, as the *extreme* Canadian cost of such insurance is but $1,125. This, on the September shipment to Liverpool *alone*, gives a loss of from $45,000 to $85,000, which loss, in the end, comes probably out of the agriculturists.*

Of course these "rates" are based upon the actual results of experience. This being so, the question at one suggests itself, What is the cause for this great *difference* of experience between Boston and Montreal? To this the unqualified answer is that it is due to a properly maintained veterinary inspection carried on systematically under proper laws and upheld by the Canadian Government, while we have nothing of the sort. To substantiate this it will perhaps be well to quote here from a letter recently received from Messrs. Endicott & Macomber, insurance agents, of Boston, Mass., who have this year employed an inspector, and who would accept no "risks" on cattle unless they had been "passed" by this examiner. On October 27, 1880, they write: "We have made this list of ours to include the whole sickly season. It shows a loss of $1\frac{1}{4}$ per cent., and would show much less had we not taken a small line on Brazilian, which ran into a gale on first day out. The loss on uninspected cattle during the same time has been upward of 6 per cent." When it is remembered that this inspection is only undertaken during the "sickly season," and to prevent the ill results arising from Texas fever alone the facts are full of significance.

As affecting the breeders of Missouri and Illinois, it may be said that in Boston, October 5, 1880, cattle for shipment were selling at the following prices: Ohio cattle, among which there is considered to be no risk of Texan contamination, 6 cents to $6\frac{1}{4}$ cents; Illinois steers, $5\frac{3}{4}$ cents; Missouri steers, $5\frac{1}{2}$ cents. That is, the Missouri farmer, besides having to pay more freight, loses about $15 per head on his steers, and he has to stand not only this severe loss, but in addition, during these months, the constant risk of having his herd contaminated, which invariably results in a heavy death loss.

The absolute remedy for this is plain, and in view of the facts as related, suggests itself, viz: Let there be enacted proper laws, with a provision for their proper execution by properly-qualified persons, which can be done without injustice to the Southern breeders, and the Western, Northern, and Eastern breeders, traders, and shippers will be protected from this source of danger to the very large commercial interests which they together represent.†

---

* It is also said to be a fact that while, even at these ruinous rates, the American companies have been losing money the Canadian and English companies have been making something.

† In a communication from Messrs. Endicott & Macomber, Boston, dated November 8, 1880, they write: "Inclosed please find report from the Allan line, * * * this shows what inspection will do." The "report," which is printed on a postal card, is as follows:

ALLAN LINE.—The cargo shipments of this line, which have arrived at the port of Liverpool and Glasgow up till this date, this season, took out 10,179 oxen; 18 horses; 11,300 sheep, which were all landed alive and in good order, with the exception of 24 oxen and 159 sheep.

MONTREAL, *October* 19, 1880.

I am perfectly willing and even anxious to give inspection its *full* value, but I honestly think that good management, and good ventilation on board ship, may have had something to do with the splendid results attained by this company. However, what one company can do in this direction, another should be able to approach. I

FOOT-AND-MOUTH DISEASE

Has been landed in Great Britain in several instances among cargoes of sheep, and once in a cargo of bullocks from the United States. This is a scheduled contagious disease, and our animals are now under restrictions because of it, which, of course, as long as the contagious pleuro-pneumonia restriction remains, does not really make any difference, and probably any measure that will provide for a *properly conducted* inspection of our cattle previous to shipment will prevent further trouble from this cause.

SHEEP SCAB

Has also been landed from the United States. A proper inspection before shipment will stop this, and thus prevent future trouble.

SWINE FEVER.

Hogs arriving from the United States are restricted on account of this disease. To devise a perfect method for preventing this needs further time and consideration.

Very respectfully,

CHARLES P. LYMAN, F. R. C. V. S.

Hon. WM. G. LE DUC,
    Commissioner of Agriculture.

---

have seen no public statement of this kind made by any other of the steamship companies.

After all, it may be that inspection deserves all the credit these gentlemen have given it, for I find by taking the figures given in Vaughan Brothers' monthly statements of the number of animals shipped to Liverpool and the number dying on the passage, that we have the following results :

In June were shipped from Boston, 5,849; of these 18 died.
In June were shipped from Montreal, 3,988; of these 26 died.
In July were shipped from Boston, 5,404; of these 39 died.
In July were shipped from Montreal, 3,985; of these 21 died.
In August were shipped from Boston, 5,488; of these 97 died.
In August were shipped from Montreal, 2,781; of these 3 died.
In September were shipped from Boston, 5,987; of these 181 died.
In September were shipped from Montreal, 4,059; of these 12 died.

It would seem from this that the steamers running from Boston have as good management and ventilation as those from Montreal, on the whole, and that given an equally healthy stock to ship from, that they are as able to show good results. Further, that the ratio of loss increases inexplainably, beginning slightly in July and running through September, unless *some* theory of special cause is accepted.

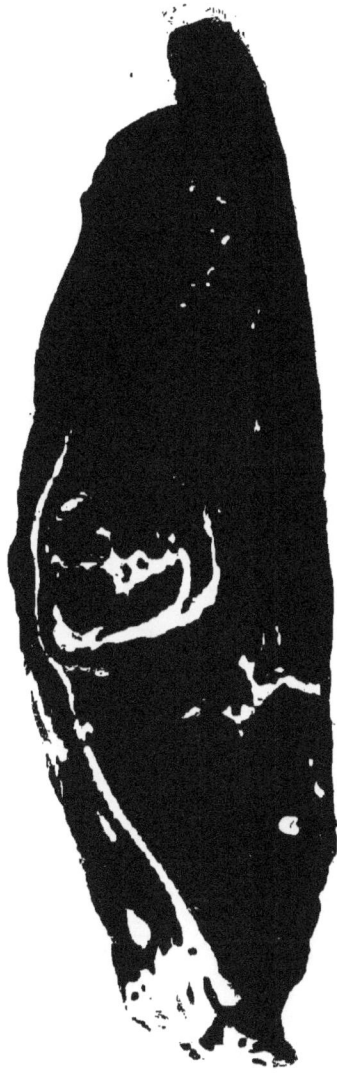

APPENDIX.

[Extract from annual report of the Veterinary Department of the Privy Council Office of Great Britain, 1879.]

The most notable event of the past year in connection with the trade in foreign animals was the removal of the United States of America from the list of countries mentioned in Part IV of the Foreign Animal Orders, wing to the landing at different times during the year of animals affected with pleuro-pneumonia, foot-and-mouth disease, and swine-fever.

My attention was first called to the existence of pleuro-pneumonia among cattle which had been landed at Liverpool from the steamship Dominion from Portland, State of Maine. It is somewhat remarkable that a mistake was made by the policeman who reported the case to the inspector of the local authority in recording the name of the port of shipment as Quebec, instead of Portland. The inquiry which was immediately instituted was commenced under the impression that the diseased animals had come from Canada, instead of the United States of America.

The circumstances were, shortly, as follows:

On January 14, I received a letter from the Veterinary Inspector of the Local Authority of Liverpool, informing me that he had forwarded for my inspection the lungs of a Canadian bullock (ex-ship Dominion from Quebec).

The bullock had been dressed in the abattoirs at Liverpool, and the Veterinary Inspector's attention had been called to the lungs, one portion of which he found to present appearances "so nearly allied to those of pleuro-pneumonia as to warrant suspicion."

My own conviction at the time was that an examination of the lungs would suffice to show that there was no ground for any suspicion. It was almost impossible that pleuro-pneumonia could have existed in Canada without having been detected, and up to the moment of receiving the letter referred to not a shadow of suspicion had been thrown upon Canadian cattle.

When the lungs were seen, however, it was at once apparent that something more than suspicion was justified. All the unmistakable marks of pleuro-pneumonia were evident, and had the animal from which the lungs had been removed been an English bullock instead of a Canadian animal, as it was then believed to be, no more trouble would have been taken in the matter. But there could be no doubt that the assertion of the existence of the disease in a bullock from Canada would be sternly denied by the Canadian authorities, who would point to the fact that no case of the disease could be found in their country. It was therefore necessary to place the matter beyond all doubt before any action could be taken. Meanwhile the diseased lungs were submitted to the inspection of all the authorities within immediate reach, and all who examined them, including Professors Simonds, Pritchard, and Axe, Messrs. Priestman, Rayment, Holmars, besides the inspectors attached to the department, unhesitatingly stated their opinion that the disease was pleuro-pneumonia. Dr. Yeo, of King's College, who had recently been engaged on behalf of the Agricultural Society in investigating the morbid anatomy of the disease, was next appealed to, not without a lingering hope that he would find on minute examination some microscopic differences between the diseased structures and the similar tissues which he had examined from English animals affected with pleuro-pneumonia, and so relieve me from a difficulty which threatened to assume considerable proportions. Before Dr. Yeo replied the difficulty had been removed by the discovery of the fact that the diseased animal formed part of a cargo from the United States, where pleuro-pneumonia was known to exist. Dr. Yeo, after a careful examination of the lungs which were sent to him, wrote:

"I regard the lung as a beautiful example of the contagious pleuro-pneumonia."

The detection of disease in the cargo brought by the Ontario afforded further evidence of its existence among cattle in the United States.

Cargoes of cattle among which pleuro-pneumonia was detected continued to arrive, and, after careful deliberation, the Lords of the Council passed an Order, on February 10, to come into force on March 4, the effect of which was to cause the slaughter of cattle from the States at the place of landing in this country.

It was probably to be expected that the importers of animals from the United States

17

would hesitate to accept as final the opinion of the inspectors of the Privy Council when that opinion was quite adverse to their interests. Accordingly, they sought the advice of three gentlemen of undoubted authority in veterinary science, the three principals of the veterinary colleges in Scotland. Two of these experts promptly decided that the disease among the cattle from the Ontario was pleuro-pneumonia; the third formed the opinion that the disease was not pleuro-pneumonia. The matter would not be referred to in this report but for the circumstance that the difference of opinion led to a question being raised in the House of Commons.

On May 12 Mr. Mundella asked the vice-president of the council if he was aware that Prof. W. Williams, of the Edinburgh Veterinary College, had written a letter to Dr. Laidlaw, veterinary pathologist, of Albany, N.Y., denying in the most emphatic terms that pleuro-pneumonia had existed in any cattle hitherto imported from the United States; whether his attention had been called to a letter of Professor Williams, dated 29th March, in which the following passage occurred: "Since first arrival of Ontario with cattle, others have arrived at Liverpool, and I have examined the lungs said by Privy-Council inspectors to have pleuro-pneumonia, and satisfied all who have seen them that no pleuro-pneumonia has arrived here from America; indeed, everybody is surprised that such a gross mistake should have been made. The last lot, seven in number, examined by me had bronchitis, with collapse of the lung, but not a trace of pleurisy nor of pneumonia, yet they were declared by the authorities in London to have typical pleuro-neupmonia. I have the specimens most carefully preserved, and am ready to show them to the whole world if necessary"; and what steps he proposed to take to satisfy himself of the correctness of those statements.

Lord George Hamilton replied that a statement of Professor Williams was forwarded to the Privy Council office by the Canadian Government last month, and upon receiving it the Privy Council requested Professor Brown, the head of the Veterinary Department, to investigate the subject. He would read the memorandum which he had drawn up, and which was sent in reply to the Canadian Government:

"On January 26 the steamship Ontario arrived at Liverpool, having on board 195 cattle and two carcases; 87 head of cattle had been thrown overboard, making the total number shipped 284. On examining one of the carcases, the inspector at Liverpool found evidence of pleuro-pneumonia, and forwarded portions of the lung to the Veterinary Department. This specimen was found to represent the characteristic indications of the contagious pleuro-pneumonia of cattle so well known in this country. By directions of the Lord President, I immediately instructed Mr. Duguid, one of the inspectors of this department, to proceed to Liverpool and report as to the condition of the animals which had been detained there. Mr. Duguid remained at Liverpool and superintended the slaughter of the cattle, and in the course of the *post-mortem* examination he detected thirteen cases of pleuro-pneumonia in various stages. Since the landing of the cattle from the Ontario, in January, cases of the disease have been detected among cattle from the United States by the inspector at Liverpool in three other cargoes, and in one cargo by the inspector at the foreign-cattle market, Deptford. Portions of the lungs taken from the diseased cattle were forwarded by the inspectors to the Veterinary Department, and I took the opportunity of submitting some of the specimens to the inspection of several experts who have made pluero-pneumonia of cattle a subject of special inquiry, and they were unanimous in their expression of opinion that the morbid changes were indicative of contagious pleuro-pneumonia. I may add that the alterations which are apparent in the lung structure in contagious pleuro-pneumonia, even in the earliest stages, are so different from those which occur in any other affection of the lungs of the ox that no competent pathologist would experience any difficulty in arriving at a correct conclusion as to the nature of the disease."

In the appendix an account is given of the number of cattle affected with pleuro-pneumonia which were landed in this country from the United States during the year. The number is considerable, and far in excess of the total number of cases of the disease which have been detected among cattle imported in the same period from the continent of Europe. This circumstance ceases to be remarkable when the widespread existence of the disease in the States is considered in connection with the fact that the extraordinary development of the cattle-trade with this country has afforded owners of infected herds an opportunity of disposing of the animals expeditiously, and in a manner much more effective than any system of isolation would be.

Further restrictions on imports from America were soon rendered necessary, in consequence of the landing in this country from the States of several cargoes of swine, among which swine-fever was detected. The existence of this disease in America, under the name of hog cholera, was too well known to admit of any discussion, and as diseased animals continued to be landed at Liverpool and Deptford, an Order of Council was passed, on May 8, to come into effect on June 2, placing swine from America in the same position as cattle. It was subsequently found necessary, in consequence of numerous cargoes of diseased swine being sent to this country during May, to bring the Order into operation at an earlier date than that originally fixed.

The slaughter of large numbers of American swine at the port of landing on account of swine-fever afforded an opportunity of obtaining specimens of flesh for examination, with the view to ascertain what proportion of the animals were infected with trichinæ. The inspectors of the Veterinary Department examined 279 separate portions of swines' flesh which were sent from Liverpool, and detected living trichinæ in three specimens.

Portions of trichinized flesh were given to two young pigs, and also to cats and rats, and the mature worm and also the encysted embryos were in this way cultivated. No doubt, therefore, existed as to the dangerous character of American pork, and a consultation on the subject took place with the medical officers of the Local Government Board; the matter was also discussed in the House of Commons, but it was not deemed expedient to prohibit the introduction of American pork into this country, for the reason that such a measure would have damaged the trade without producing any satisfactory results. A large proportion of the objectionable meat would have been sent to this country by a circuitous route, and thus the object of the restriction would have been defeated; besides which trichinosis among swine is known to exist in Germany, and it probably exists in other exporting countries, so that nothing short of total prohibition of swine flesh in all forms from all foreign sources would have been effectual. The possibility of our own swine being to some extent infected with trichinæ has been suggested; the result, however, of many examinations has, up to this time, been negative.

American sheep were the next animals to be brought within the provisions of a special Order of Council. On July 4, the Inspector of the Privy Council at Liverpool reported that he had detected foot-and-mouth disease in a cargo of sheep brought from Boston and landed at Liverpool on July 3.

The Chief Inspector was instructed to proceed to Liverpool and examine the diseased animals, and in the course of his inspection he detected ten cases of the disease in various stages.

An Order of Council was accordingly passed, on November 4, to come into operation on November 24, placing sheep in the same position as cattle and swine from the United States.

No information of the existence of foot-and-mouth disease among animals in the United States of America had been communicated to the Veterinary Department, but it is worthy of remark that in the report of the Minister of Agriculture, at Washington, in answer to a Senate resolution of February 21, 1878, requiring information respecting the prevalence of diseases among swine and other domestic animals in the States, one of the writers describes a disease, which he calls "murrain," in the following terms:

"The disease most prevalent among cattle is murrain. It is characterized by small vesicles in the mouth, on lips, gums, and tongue, with drivelings of saliva, often causing inability to eat or drink. These symptoms are accompanied with fever, swelling of the udder, and lameness."

The writer is not a veterinary surgeon, and he evidently describes in his letter more than one disease under the term murrain; but the above record of symptoms might be copied literally in describing an ordinary case of foot-and-mouth disease in this country.

The Order of Council which provided for the slaughter of American sheep at a foreign-animals' wharf practically completed the exclusion of American animals from Part IV of the foreign animals order. No injury, however, appears to have been done to the trade by this action, and, indeed, so far as the consumer is concerned, it does not appear to be of much consequence whether foreign animals were imported under the provisions of Part II or Part IV of the Order. The object of their introduction into the country is that of adding to the food supply; and experience tends to show that slaughter at the place of landing has not seriously interfered with this object.

In the last report reference was made to the enormous losses which were caused by the hardships of the trans-Atlantic passage, and it is, perhaps, not surprising, considering the extraordinary weather of 1879, that the number of animals lost in transit was considerably larger than in the previous year, as the following analysis of the returns will show:

From Canada there were landed in 1879 at the ports of Bristol, Glasgow, Liverpool, and London 157 cargoes of animals, consisting of 25,185 cattle, 73,913 sheep, 3,663 swine, of which, 154 cattle, 1,623 sheep, and 249 swine were thrown overboard during the voyage; 21 cattle, 226 sheep, and 3 swine were landed dead, and 4 cattle and 61 sheep had to be slaughtered at the place of landing, owing to injuries received in transit.

From the United States there were landed in 1879 at the ports of Bristol, Cardiff, Glasgow, Grimsby, Hartlepool, Hull, Leith, Liverpool, London, Newcastle-upon-Tyne, South Shields, and Southampton 535 cargoes of animals, consisting of 76,117 cattle, 119,350 sheep, and 15,180 swine, of which 3,140 cattle, 5,915 sheep, and 2,943 swine were thrown overboard on the voyage; 221 cattle, 386 sheep, and 392 swine were landed dead; and

93 cattle, 167 sheep, and 130 swine were so much injured that it was necessary to slaughter them at the place of landing.

Thus it appears that 14,024 animals were thrown overboard, 1,249 were landed dead, and 455 were so much injured or exhausted that they were killed at the place of landing; making a total number of 15,728 animals which were either lost on the passage or so much injured that it was necessary to slaughter them immediately on landing.

Notwithstanding the increased restrictions on importation, the number of foreign animals imported was larger in 1879 than in the previous year, the total from all countries out of the United Kingdom being 1,241,847 as against 1,200,323 in 1878. From European countries we received 143,187 cattle, 750,469 sheep, 32,591 swine; from Canada, 25,185 cattle, 73,913 sheep, 3,663 swine; from the United States of America, 76,117 cattle, 119,350 sheep, 15,180 swine; from the Channel Islands, 2,151 cattle only; from other countries, 12 cattle, 22 sheep, 7 swine.

From Ireland we received 641,370 cattle, 673,371 sheep, 429,663 swine.

The total from all sources was 2,986,251 animals in 1879 against 3,043,090 in 1878.

There were landed in Great Britain during 1879, from places out of the United Kingdom, exclusive of the Channel Islands, 2,671 cargoes of animals, consisting of 244,501 cattle, 973,754 sheep, 51,441 swine. In 122 cargoes the inspectors detected disease among the animals on landing in this country. The diseased cargoes came from the following countries: Belgium, 46 cargoes, of which 6 cargoes, consisting of 3,141 sheep, contained 8 sheep affected with foot-and-mouth disease and 68 sheep affected with sheep-scab. France, 27 cargoes, of which 2 cargoes, consisting of 25 cattle, 30 swine, contained 1 cattle affected with pleuro-pneumonia and 20 swine affected with foot-and-mouth disease. Germany, 496 cargoes, of which 21 cargoes, consisting of 312 cattle, 28,277 sheep, contained 29 sheep affected with foot-and-mouth disease and 496 sheep affected with sheep-scab. The Netherlands, 659 cargoes, of which 21 cargoes, consisting of 1,830 cattle, 11,076 sheep, 1,079 swine, contained 9 cattle affected with pleuro-pneumonia, 1 head of cattle, 7 sheep, and 64 swine affected with foot-and-mouth disease, and 83 sheep affected with sheep-scab. Canada, 157 cargoes, of which 3 cargoes, consisting of 339 cattle, 1,746 sheep, 180 swine, contained 13 sheep affected with sheep-scab. The United States of America, 535 cargoes, of which 69 cargoes, consisting of 13,301 cattle, 8,553 sheep, contained 137 cattle affected with pleuro-pneumonia, 33 sheep affected with foot-and-mouth disease, and 37 sheep affected with sheep-scab.

In addition to the Orders which were in force on January 1, 1879, it was found necessary to pass several Orders in the course of the year, either for the purpose of amending certain provisions in existing Orders or dealing with new conditions.

On the 1st of January, 1879, the new regulations relating to the importation of foreign animals, which had been enacted by the Contagious Diseases (animals) Act, 1878, and contained in the Foreign Animals Order (dated the 6th of December, 1878, and numbered 422), came into operation. As stated in the report for the year 1878, the act of 1878 provides that the foreign animals are to be landed only at a foreign-animals' wharf, and are to be there slaughtered, except such animals from such countries as may be from time to time specially prohibited or excepted by Order of Council. The principal features of the provisions of the Foreign Animals Order will be treated hereafter under the heading *orders relating to importation.*

Orders relating to Importation.—Before noticing the Orders that were issued during 1879 on this subject, it would be well to notice the more salient points of the provisions of the Foreign Animals Order No. 452, which, as before stated, came into operation on the 1st of January, 1879.

The act of 1878 provided that foreign animals should only be landed in a part of a port, to be called a foreign-animals' wharf, out of which wharf they were not to be moved alive, unless the Privy Council by Order absolutely prohibited their being landed, or specially exempted them from the operation of those provisions of the act.

The Foreign Animals Order first, prohibited the landing of animals brought from the following countries: The Austrian-Hungarian Empire, The Dominions of the King of the Hellenes, The Dominions of the King of Italy, The Principality of Montenegro, The Principality of Roumania, The Dominions of the Emperor of Russia, The Dominions of the Sultan, including The Provinces of Bosnia and Herzegovina.

Secondly, sets forth the ports which had parts defined as foreign-animals' wharves, namely, Goole, Grimsby, Hartlepool, London, Plymouth, Sunderland, and laid down regulations as to the time of the slaughter of animals landed in those wharves.

Thirdly, provided for the quarantine of foreign animals at a part of the port of Southampton defined as a foreign-animals' quarantine station.

Fourthly, exempted animals from compulsory slaughter if brought from the following countries: Her Majesty's Possessions in North America, the United States of America, Denmark, Norway, Sweden, Spain, Portugal. Animals from these countries were to be landed at a place of landing approved by the Privy Council within one of the following ports: Bristol, Cardiff, Falmouth, Glasgow, Goole, Granton, Grimsby, Hartlepool, Leith, Liverpool, London, Newcastle-upon-Tyne, Plymouth, Portsmouth, Southampton, Sunderland, Weymouth. And general regulations were framed as to the slaughter and disposal of such animals if found diseased, and as to their ceasing to be deemed foreign animals if, after detention for not less than twelve hours, the whole cargo was certified by an inspector of the Privy Council to be free from disease.

Fifthly. Animals brought from the Channel Islands were exempted from compulsory slaughter, and subjected to the regulations last mentioned.

Sixthly. Animals brought from the Isle of Man were exempted from all restrictions relating to importation.

The first Order passed during the year 1879, relating to importations, was that dated the 10th of February, which ordered that from and after the 3d day of March, then next, cattle brought from the United States of America should cease to be exempted from the regulations regarding slaughter; or, in other words provided that they should be landed in a foreign-animals' wharf for slaughter.

On the 13th of February an Order was passed providing that cows or goats taken on board a vessel in Great Britain for the purpose of supplying the passengers or crew with milk on a voyage were not, on being landed in Great Britain at the end of the voyage, to be deemed foreign animals, if the Customs were, before the same were landed, satisfied that they had been taken from Great Britain and had not been landed in a foreign country, and had not been in contact with any foreign animal.

On the 28th of February a foreign-animals' wharf was defined at the Wallasey landing-stage at Birkenhead in the port of Liverpool. This became necessary in consequence of the passing of the before-mentioned order No. 467, relating to cattle from the United States of America.

Middlesbrough was opened for the landing of foreign animals for slaughter by having a foreign-animals' wharf on the south side of the river Tees, near Commercial street, defined by Order dated the 25th of March. Hull was also opened for animals for slaughter by having a foreign-animals' wharf defined by Order dated March 25, and subsequently for animals not subject to slaughter or to quarantine, by Order dated the 28th of March.

Owing to the difficulty of carrying on the London-American cattle-trade in consequence of the only foreign-animals' wharf (the foreign-cattle market at Deptford) being situate high up the river, a temporary Order, to continue in force for two months, was passed on the 3d of April, permitting, from and after the 4th of that month, cattle brought from the United States of America to the port of London to be transshipped in the Victoria docks for conveyance to that market. This privilege was extended to American cattle transshipped in the Millwall docks by Order of Council dated the 8th of May. Just before the two last-mentioned Orders expired, another Order was passed on the 29th of May, to take effect on the 4th of June, permitting animals (this Order did not confine the transshipment to cattle, as at that time American swine were also obliged to be slaughtered on landing) brought from the United States of America to the port of London to be transshipped in the river Thames, or in any dock within the port of London approved by the Privy Council, for conveyance to Deptford. This latter Order remained in force at the end of the year.

At the same time another Order was passed, also to take effect on the 4th of June, formally revoking the temporary Orders Nos. 475 and 481.

Difficulty having also been experienced at the ports of Hull and Glasgow in carrying on the trade in animals from America, owing to the great depth of water drawn by the vessels engaged in the trade, Orders were passed, on the 14th of May, permitting, from and after that date, animals brought to the port of Hull from the United States to be trans-shipped in the river Humber or in the Albert dock for conveyance to the foreign-animals' wharf at Citadel estate, and, on the 15th of August, permitting, from and after the 16th of that month, the transshipment of such animals brought to the port of Glasgow, in the Firth of Clyde or in the river Clyde for conveyance to the foreign-animals' wharf at Yorkhill Wharf.

Owing to the accommodation at the Wallasey landing-stage at Birkenhead being found inadequate for the trade, the wharf was enlarged. It therefore became necessary to revoke the former defining Order, No. 470, and to redefine the wharf. Two Orders were accordingly passed, on the 8th of April, to effect that object.

Although Goole was inserted in the foreign-animals Order No. 452 as a port having a foreign-animals' wharf, it was not, in consequence of the inadequate accommodation provided, until the 8th of April that the wharf was finally approved and the Order defining it was passed.

Several cargoes of swine affected with swine-fever having arrived from America, an Order of Council was issued on the 8th of May, providing, in effect, that swine brought from the United States of America should be subject to the same restrictions as cattle, namely, that they should be landed in a foreign-animals' wharf for slaughter. The Order was to have come into force from the 1st of June, but, owing to other diseased cargoes arriving, that date was, by a subsequent Order passed on the 13th of May, altered to the 16th of May.

The authorities at the ports of Bristol and Cardiff desiring to import American cattle and swine applied to have parts defined as foreign-animals' wharves. Accordingly, on the 13th of May, two Orders of Council were passed, one defining a wharf at Avonmouth Dock, in the port of Bristol, the other defining a wharf at the Roath Basin of the Bute Docks, in the port of Cardiff, as foreign-animals' wharves.

The American trade increasing at Liverpool, it was again found necessary to provide further accommodation. This necessitated the issuing of the following Orders: On the 16th of May the order of the 8th of April, No. 477, was revoked, and another defining Order was passed redefining the wharf as again enlarged at the Wallasey landing-stage at Birkenhead, and defining also a second foreign-animals' wharf at the Woodside landing-stage at Birkenhead. On the 4th of July another foreign-animals' wharf was defined on the Liverpool side of the Mersey, known as Huskisson Branch Dock No. 2; and, finally, on the 28th of July, still further accommodation having been found necessary, the two Orders then in force, Nos. 488 and 498, were rescinded, and the Order which remained in force to the end of the year, defining all three wharves, was passed.

On the 23d of May an Order was issued extending the time from ten days to fourteen days within which animals in foreign-animals' wharves must be slaughtered. This regulation came into operation on the 25th of May.

On the 29th of May the usual Annual Order was passed providing for the landing, from the 31st of May to the end of the year, of cattle from the provinces of Schleswig and Holstein, in Germany, at a foreign-animals' wharf for slaughter. This was necessary in consequence of cattle from the German Empire being otherwise still prohibited.

South Shields had a foreign-animals' wharf defined at Tyne Dock by Order dated the 13th of June. The wharf, however, not proving sufficiently large for the trade, that Order was revoked, and a new Order issued redefining the same wharf with a further area on the 15th of August.

Glasgow had a foreign-animals' wharf defined at Yorkhill Wharf by Order on the 23d of June, but which was revoked on the 27th of October, and the wharf was redefined on the latter date.

It having been decided by the admiralty that the Royal William Victualling Yard at Plymouth, which has been defined as a foreign-animals' wharf by Order No. 459, should be used exclusively for naval purposes, that Order was revoked on the 21st of July, and on the same day another Order was passed defining as foreign-animals' wharves, for naval purposes only, the Royal William Victualling Yard at Plymouth and the Royal Clarence Victualling Yard at Portsmouth.

On the 17th of September a second foreign-animals' wharf for the port of Bristol was defined at the Cumberland Tidal Basin in the town of Bristol.

The port of Harwich was opened for the importation of foreign-animals not subject to slaughter or to quarantine on the 11th of October.

Barrow-in-Furness had a foreign-animals' wharf defined at Ramsden Dock on the 11th of October.

On the 4th of November an Order of Council was passed ordering sheep to be landed in a foreign-animals' wharf for slaughter if brought from the United States of America. The Order took effect from the 23d of November, and was issued in consequence of sheep from that country having been found on landing to be affected with foot-and-mouth disease.

A foreign-animals' wharf was defined at Southampton on the Southampton Dock Company's premises, known as the Extension Quay, on the 7th of November; and

The Order of Council defining a foreign-animals' wharf at Middlesbrough, passed on the 25th of March, No. 473, was revoked, and that port was opened for the importation of foreign animals not subject to slaughter or to quarantine, by Order dated the 29th of November.

The only other Orders affecting importation passed during the year 1879 were the revocation Order, No. 522 (revoking all former Orders except such local Orders as it was intended should remain in force, and the general Order relating to dairies and cow-sheds), and the Animals' Order, No. 523, consolidating all General Orders in force (except the General Order relating to dairies and cow-sheds). Both these Orders are further noticed, under the heading *consolidating orders.*

The following statement will show the places where foreign animals could be landed on the 31st of December, 1879:

Barrow-in-Furness.—Barrow-in-Furness has one foreign-animals' wharf: (*a*) Ramsden Dock (O. C. 514); but is not open for animals not for slaughter.

Bristol.—Bristol has two foreign-animal wharves: (*a*) Avonmouth Dock (O. C. 484); (*b*) Cumberland Tidal Basin (O. C. 512); and has two landing-places for animals not for slaughter: (1) Railway Dock, (2) Avonmouth Dock.

Cardiff.—Cardiff has one foreign-animals' wharf: (*a*) Roath Basin (O. C. 485); but is not open for animals not for slaughter.

Falmouth.—Falmouth has not a foreign-animals' wharf, but has one landing-place for animals not for slaughter, (1) Penryn Wharf.

Glasgow.—Glasgow has one foreign-animals' wharf: (*a*) Yorkhill Wharf (O. C. 516); and has one landing-place for animals not for slaughter, (1) Plantation Quay.

Goole.—Goole has one foreign-animals' wharf: (*a*) Railway Dock (O. C. 478); but is not open for animals not for slaughter.

Granton.—Granton has not a foreign-animals' wharf, but has two landing-places for animals not for slaughter, (1) Granton Harbor, (2) Granton Quay.

Grimsby.—Grimsby has one foreign-animals' wharf: (*a*) the 70-foot lock of the Royal Dock (O. C. 456); and has one landing-place for animals not for slaughter, (1) Royal Dock.

Hartlepool.—Hartlepool has one foreign-animals' wharf: (*a*) west side of the Jackson Dock (O. C. 457); and has one landing-place for animals not for slaughter, (1) Southeast corner of the Jackson Dock.

Harwich.—Harwich has not a foreign-animals' wharf, but has one landing-place for animals not for slaughter: (1) Great Eastern Railway Company's Pier.

Hull.—Hull has one foreign-animals' wharf: (*a*) Citadel Estate (O. C. 472); and has two landing-places for animals not for slaughter: (1) Albert Dock; (2) Quay-wall of Albert Dock.

Leith.—Leith has not a foreign-animals' wharf, but has two landing-places for animals not for slaughter: (1) Albert Dock; (2) Victoria Dock.

Liverpool.—Liverpool has three foreign-animals' wharves (O. C. 505): (*a*) Huskisson Branch Dock No. 2. Liverpool; (*b*) Wallasey landing-stage, Birkenhead; (*c*) Woodside landing-stage, Birkenhead; and has six landing-places for animals not for slaughter. (For all animals:) (1) Canada Dock, Liverpool; (2) shed on the north side of the Alfred Dock, Birkenhead; (3) inclosed space on the east of the before-mentioned shed, Birkenhead; (4) inclosed space on the northeast corner of the Great Float, Birkenhead. (For animals other than cattle:) (5) Southern end of the Wallasey landing-stage, Birkenhead; (6) sheds No. 4. No. 6, and No. 8, on the south side of the Wallasey Dock, Birkenhead.

London.—London has one foreign-animals' wharf: (*a*) Foreign Cattle Market, Deptford (O. C. 458), and has three landing-places for animals not for slaughter: (1) Brown's Wharf; (2) Victoria Docks; (3) Thames Haven.

Middlesbrough.—Middlesbrough has not a foreign-animals' wharf, but has one landing-place for animals not for slaughter: (1) Taylor's Wharf.

Newcastle-upon-Tyne.—Newcastle-upon-Tyne has not a foreign-animals' wharf, but has one landing-place for animals not for slaughter: (1) Legal Quay.

Plymouth.—Plymouth has one foreign-animals' wharf, for naval purposes only: (*a*) Royal William Victualling Yard (O. C. 502); and has four landing-places for animals not for slaughter: (1) Commercial Wharf; (2) Keyham Dock Yard; (3) Mill Bay; (4) Sutton Wharf.

Portsmouth.—Portsmouth has one foreign-animals' wharf for naval purposes only: (*a*) Royal Clarence Victualling Yard (O. C. 502); and has one landing-place for animals not for slaughter: (1) Chamber Dock.

Southampton.—Southampton has one foreign-animals' wharf: (*a*) Extension Quay (O. C. 518); and has a foreign-animals' quarantine station: (*b*) Southern side of the Close Dock (O. C. 461); and has one landing-place for animals not for slaughter: (1) Southampton Docks.

South Shields.—South Shields has one foreign-animals' wharf: (*a*) Tyne Dock (O. C. 509); but is not open for animals not for slaughter.

Sunderland.—Sunderland has one foreign-animals' wharf: (*a*) North Half Tide Basin (O. C. 460); and has one landing-place for animals not for slaughter: (1) Hudson Dock North.

Weymouth.—Weymouth has not a foreign-animals' wharf, but has one landing-place for animals not for slaughter: (1.) Harbour Quay.

DISEASES AMONG FOREIGN ANIMALS LANDED IN GREAT BRITAIN.

The diseases which were detected by the Inspectors of the Privy Council stationed at the ports in Great Britain among foreign animals landed in this country during 1879 were pleuro-pneumonia, foot-and-mouth disease, sheep-scab, and swine-fever.

The diseased animals came from Canada, the United States of America, Belgium, France, Germany, and the Netherlands.

Pleuro-pneumonia.—The first cases of pleuro-pneumonia among foreign stock were detected by the inspector at Liverpool, in the latter part of January. The ship Ontario, from Portland, State of Maine, landed 197 cattle at Liverpool in January; two dead cattle were also landed; and on making a post-mortem of one of the carcasses the inspector detected the marked appearance indicative of pleuro-pneumonia. He forwarded portions of the lungs to this department, and an examination of the parts sent up was made by the officers of the department, when all the post-mortem appearances of pleuro-pneumonia, as observed in animals afflicted with that disease in this country, were found to exist. The cargo was therefore detained, and the assistant inspector of the department was instructed to proceed to Liverpool to assist the inspector at that port in his inspection of the living animals, and to report fully on the subject.

At this period no proper accommodation existed at the port of Liverpool for either the lairage or slaughter of foreign animals ; these cattle had been placed in one of the sheds at the Huskisson Dock, where it would have been practically impossible to have slaughtered them ; permission was therefore given for the removal of the apparently healthy cattle to the abattoir, where a further examination of them was made and the post-mortem appearances of all their lungs carefully noted, when it was found that a large number of the animals were suffering from interlobular emphysema, and the ordinary inflammatory diseases of the respiratory organs, viz., bronchitis, pneumonia, and pleurisy, the results of cold and exposure.

In twelve of the cattle the distinctive appearances of pleuro-pneumonia were observed.

On February 9 the disease was detected in a cargo of cattle which arrived in the Istrian from Boston, and on the following day an Order of Council was passed, which came into force on March 4, subjecting cattle from the United States to slaughter at the ports of landing.

With a view, however, to assist in the detection of any cases of pleuro-pneumonia which might arrive prior to this Order coming into operation the assistant inspector remained at Liverpool.

It occasionally happened that only one animal in a cargo was found diseased, but on the 16th of December the Illyrian arrived at Liverpool from Boston having 69 cattle on board ; these animals were all slaughtered in the foreign-animals' wharf, and their lungs were examined by the inspector at the port, when pleuro-pneumonia was detected in no less than twelve cases. From the date of the detection of the first cases of pleuro-pneumonia among American cattle on January 26th to December 31, 137 cases of the disease have been reported among cattle forming part of 57 cargoes.

Foot-and-mouth disease.—A noticeable fact in regard to this disease is that it appears to have prevailed to a very small extent on the continent of Europe. During the past year animals affected with foot-and-mouth disease have been received from Belgium, Holland, France, Germany, and the United States of America, and it appears to have chiefly manifested itself among sheep and swine, only one head of cattle which arrived from Harlingen having been found to be affected with that disease. The most important point in connection with this affection is the fact of its detection among sheep which arrived at the port of Liverpool from the United States of America, a country in which the existence of that disease does not appear to have been generally recognized.

On July 3 the steamship Bulgarian, from Boston, arrived at Liverpool with 1,307 sheep ; on the following day they were examined by the inspector at that port, who detained the whole cargo on the suspicion that a certain number of them were affected with foot-and-mouth disease, and immediately communicated with the department. The chief inspector was instructed to proceed to Liverpool and report on the condition of these animals. An examination was made of the whole of the sheep, which resulted in the detection of 10 cases of foot-and-mouth disease. Some of the animals had evidently been affected in their feet for many days, while others had the disease in the early stage, recently ruptured vesicles between the claws being observable, and one which was in this condition was also affected in the mouth. As this was the first cargo of animals from America among which foot-and-mouth disease had been detected, it was considered desirable, in order to establish the true nature of the disease, to communicate it, if possible, to a healthy sheep in this country. For this purpose the feet of those animals which had vesicles upon them were sent to Professor Simmonds, the principal of the Royal Veterinary College, who succeeded in producing the disease by inoculation in a healthy sheep which had been in the college for many weeks, a fact which was communicated by Professor Simmonds to the Royal Agricultural Society at a meeting held in the following month.

Other cargoes of sheep containing affected animals were landed in Liverpool in the months of September and October, the feet of which were sent to the department by the inspector at the port, and in every instance there was abundant evidence of their having been affected with foot-and-mouth disease, in consequence of which all the sheep in these several cargoes were slaughtered at the port of landing.

In all, six cargoes of sheep in which cases of foot-and-mouth disease were detected arrived from the United States. An Order of Council was passed on November 4 and came into operation on November 23, which subjected sheep from that country to slaughter on landing.

Altogether during the past year 162 foreign animals, namely, 1 head of cattle, 77 sheep, and 84 swine, were found by the inspectors of the Privy Council at the various ports to be affected with foot-and-mouth disease. The number is the smallest which has been recorded since the year 1871.

Sheep-scab.—Cases of this disease have been detected in animals brought from Belgium, Germany, the Netherlands, the United States, and Canada. All the diseased sheep and those brought in the same vessel were slaughtered at the ports of landing.

The total number of cases of scab which were detected among foreign sheep during the year 1879 was 697. Of these, 13 came from Canada and 37 from the United States; the remainder from Germany, Belgium, and the Netherlands.

Swine-fever.—Some affected with this disease have occasionally been landed in this country from the continent of Europe, and when detected the diseased animals have been slaughtered and destroyed at the place of landing, under the supervision of the inspectors of the Privy Council. The number of cases has, however, been comparatively few, and it was not until this year that the necessity has arisen for ordering the slaughter of swine on account of this disease.

Swine-fever, which is generally recognized under the name of "hog cholera" in America, has been known to exist in that country for many years; and in a paper which was issued by the Department of Agriculture at Washington, dated February 26, 1878, it was stated that out of 2,417 counties in the States and Territories of the United States, returns had been received from 1.125 counties, which showed that out of 18,987,342 swine in those counties, 2,599,542 had become affected with "hog cholera," and that the money value of the losses amounted to no less a sum than $10,091,483 annually. With a disease so extensively prevalent among swine in the United States, it was only to be expected that at some early date animals affected with that disease would arrive in this country. Accordingly, as soon as a trade in swine between that country and the United Kingdom became established, it was found that diseased swine were being exported to this country.

On April 30 the steamship Antonio, from Philadelphia, having on board 334 swine, arrived in the port of Liverpool; she had originally shipped 444, of which 110 had died and had been thrown overboard, and 59 others which were dying presented all the symptoms of swine-fever; the whole cargo was therefore detained by the inspector of the port. On the following day the assistant inspector of the department proceeded to Liverpool and made an inspection of the living diseased animals and a post-mortem examination of several others, and ascertained that they had been suffering from swine-fever in a most severe form. The swine had been landed at Woodside, Birkenhead, where no proper arrangements had at that time been provided for their slaughter and dressing; and it having been represented to the Privy Council that under these circumstances great delay must necessarily arise if the slaughter was carried out at the landing place, permission was given for the removal of those which the inspector at the port pronounced to be healthy to the abattoir at Birkenhead. This was carried out under the immediate supervision of an officer of the Local Authority, while the carcasses of all the diseased animals were destroyed at a bone-boiling yard.

Other cargoes of diseased American swine having arrived in rapid succession, an Order of Council was passed on May 8, subjecting swine from the United States to slaughter on landing, after June 1. Meanwhile further cargoes of diseased animals having arrived, article 1 of that Order was revoked by an Order of Council passed May 13, by which the date of their compulsory slaughter was altered from June 2 to May 17.

A cargo of swine, consisting of 567 animals, arrived in the steamship Viking at the Victoria Docks, from Canada, on November 14; 42 of them were found to be affected with swine-fever. The inspector brought portions of the intestines of some of the animals which had been slaughtered to the department for examination, and it was apparent that the parts had been taken from animals affected with swine-fever.

The assistant inspector of the department subsequently examined the animals, and found confirmatory evidence of the existence of the disease.

The diseased swine were all slaughtered at the landing place, and those apparently healthy were removed to Deptford for slaughter in the foreign-animal wharf.

On December 13 a cargo of swine, among which swine-fever was detected, arrived from Montreal, Canada, at Glasgow; all these animals were slaughtered at the landing-place. No cases of this disease have been detected among swine received from the continent during the past year.

Altogether there have been landed during the year 1,044 animals affected with swine-fever. Of these, 974 came from the United States and 70 from Canada.

DISEASES WHICH HAVE EXISTED AMONG ANIMALS IN FOREIGN COUNTRIES IN 1879.

AMERICA.

HER MAJESTY'S POSSESSIONS IN NORTH AMERICA, AND THE UNITED STATES OF AMERICA.

No information of the existence of diseases among animals in Canada has been received during the year 1879, but the inspectors at English ports detected 13 sheep affected with sheep-scab, and 70 swine affected with swine-fever, on being landed in this country from Canadian ports.

Animals imported from Canada, if healthy, are not subject to slaughter at the port of landing. During 1879 there were landed 25,185 cattle, 73,913 sheep, and 3,663 swine from Canada. In 1878 the number was 17,989 cattle, 40,132 sheep, and 1,614 swine.

The Canadian Government has prohibited the importation of cattle from the United States into the provinces of Ontario, Quebec, Nova Scotia, and Prince Edward Island. This Order remained in force at the end of the year.

Since the United States cattle have been slaughtered at the ports of debarkation in this country a considerable amount of interest has been aroused in the States in reference to the extent of the prevalence of pleuro-pneumonia among American cattle, and the veterinary department has received numerous papers from time to time from Her Majesty's minister at Washington, giving a detailed description of several outbreaks of that disease, and among the papers received is a report issued by the Commissioner of Agriculture, dated November, 1878, in which are the following statements:

"One of the most dreaded contagious diseases known among cattle is that of pleuro-pneumonia, or lung-fever. It was brought to this country as early as the year 1843, and has since prevailed to a greater or less extent in several of the Eastern and a few of the Southern States. It made its appearance about a century ago in Central Europe, and has since spread to most European countries. With the exception of rinderpest, it is the most dreaded and destructive disease known among cattle. Unlike Texas cattle-fever, which is controlled in our more northern latitudes by the appearance of frost, this disease knows no limitation by winter or summer, cold or heat, rain or drought, high or low latitudes. It is the most insidious of all plagues, for the poison may be retained in a system for a period of one or two months, or even for a longer period, in a latent form, and the infected animal in the mean time may be transported from one end of the continent to the other in apparent good health, yet all the while carrying and scattering the seeds of this dreaded pestilence. Since the appearance of this affection on our shores it has prevailed at different times in the States of Massachusetts, Connecticut, New York, New Jersey, Pennsylvania, Maryland, Delaware, Virginia, and in the District of Columbia. It has recently shown itself at two points in Virginia (Alexandria and Lynchburg), where it was recently prevailing in a virulent form.   *   *   *   *   *

"The interests involved in this case are of so vast a character, and of such overshadowing importance both to the farming and commercial interests of the country, as to require the active intervention of the Federal Government for their protection. And for this reason the considerate attention of Congress is respectfully asked to this important matter."

In addition to this statement on the part of the Minister of Agriculture, accounts of the appearance of the disease in several of those States have been received from Her Majesty's minister at Washington, and outbreaks of a very fatal character have been referred to, more particularly in the States of New York, New Jersey, Pennsylvania, and Virginia. It also appears that several of these States have issued through their legislatures most stringent regulations for suppressing this disease, including the slaughter of diseased cattle and the inspection and quarantine of cattle imported from a neighboring State.

The power, however, to stop importation from a neighboring State has been disputed, and a decision has been rendered by the supreme court of the State of Illinois, as to the right of a State to protect itself from contagious diseases, that all State laws interfering with the free interchange of commerce between the different States are contrary to the Constitution of the United States, and show that any legislation for the purpose of suppressing any contagious diseases among cattle, to be effective, must emanate from the Congress of the United States.

On February 1, the American Government issued a circular to the collectors of customs in the United States, ordering that all cattle should be inspected before embarkation to Great Britain. A notice was also issued to the collectors of customs on March 7, ordering that neat cattle from England should not be landed until otherwise ordered ; this prohibition was, however, modified in a circular which was issued on July 19, which stated that neat cattle from Europe would be admitted after a quarantine of ninety days.

A circular was issued on November 3, 1879, which came into effect on December 1, 1879, prohibiting the importation of neat cattle from Canada.

At the commencement of the year 1879, animals from the United States were not subject to slaughter on landing, but owing to the detection of pleuro-pneumonia among cattle, foot-and-mouth disease in sheep, and swine-fever in pigs, all animals from that country are now subject to slaughter at the port of landing. During 1879, there were imported from the United States 76,117 cattle, 119,350 sheep, and 15,180 swine, of which 137 cattle were affected with pleuro-pneumonia, 33 sheep with foot-and-mouth disease, 37 with sheep-scab, and 974 pigs with swine-fever. In 1878 the imports from the United States were 68,450 cattle, 43,940 sheep, and 16,321 swine.

CORRESPONDENCE CONNECTED WITH THE DETECTION OF PLEURO-PNEUMONIA AMONG CATTLE LANDED IN GREAT BRITAIN FROM THE UNITED STATES OF AMERICA.

No. 1.

Telegram from the Marquis of Salisbury to Her Majesty's minister at Washington, 30th January, 1879.

Pleuro-pneumonia having been detected in a cargo of cattle on board the ship Ontario, from Portland, Her Majesty's government is consequently considering whether it can retain the United States under the exemption of Part IV of the fifth schedule of the act of 1878.

No 2.

Letter from Sir E. Thornton to the Marquis of Salisbury.

WASHINGTON, *February* 3, 1879.

MY LORD : On the receipt of your Lordship's telegram of the 30th ultimo, informing me that pleuro-pneumonia had been detected in a cargo of cattle on board the ship Ontario, from Portland, and that Her Majesty's government was consequently considering whether it could retain the United States under the exemption of Part IV of the fifth Schedule of the Act of 1878, I called upon Mr. Evarts and communicated to him the contents of your telegram. He had also received one to the same effect from the United States Minister in London. He said that the information had taken him by surprise and that he had not yet made complete inquiries upon the subject. With regard to the cases of pleuro-pneumonia which had been discovered on board the Ontario, he thought it very probable that the animals had contracted the disease during the voyage and that it had been caused by bad ventilation and exposure to rough weather. He believed that there were some cases of it in different parts of the United States, but that a few always existed. They were, however, isolated cases, and there was no ground whatever for supposing that the disease was epidemic. He added that measures had now been taken for the inspection of cattle for export at the different ports of the United States, and, as it was not in the interest of the owners to ship diseased cattle, they would certainly be careful to avoid doing so. Nothing, however, could prevent isolated cases of disease contracted on board of ship ; but inspection on arrival at the port of destination, and slaughter in case of need, would preclude any danger of the spreading of the disease. He expressed his opinion that it would be hardly justifiable to stop so great a trade and to prevent the supply of food from reaching Great Britain, on account of a few isolated cases of pleuro-pneumonia, which in this country was not considered contagious.

Before I saw Mr. Evarts he had sent me a short note, a copy of which I have the honor to inclose, informing me that an agent of the British Government had been for some days past at New York and Alexandria, and had reported to the Canadian Government the existence of pleuro-pneumonia among cattle. I had not then received his note, but he told me its contents, and asked me whether I could give him any information with regard to the agent in question. I was obliged to acknowledge that I had neither seen nor heard of him.

The next morning I addressed an official note to Mr. Evarts, transmitting him a copy of your Lordship's telegram of 30th ultimo.

I also received on that morning a private letter from the acting consul at Philadelphia, of which, and of its inclosure, I have the honor to inclose a copy. From this it appears that Prof. D. McEachran, Veterinary Inspector of Canada, had been sent by the Government of the Dominion to inspect cattle in this country, and was doubtless the person to whom Mr. Evarts had alluded. It would appear that he ascertained that there had been many cases of the disease in Virginia and that he discovered that it prevailed to a great and severe extent in a large cow-house near Brooklyn, Long Island.

On the 1st instant I again called upon Mr. Evarts and read to him the greater part of Mr. Crump's and Dr. Gadsden's letters. He still, however, expressed his opinion that these cases did not affect the general cattle of the country, and particularly those which were exported.

Mr. Evarts informed me that he had made inquiries with regard to the cargo of the Ontario. It appeared that the bulk of the cargo were American cattle, but a few, about twenty-two, were Canadian. He did not know among which of these the cases of pleuro-pneumonia had been discovered. When these cattle were about to be shipped the collector of customs had offered to order an inspection of them and provide them with a certificate, but their owner declined an inspection, on the ground that a certificate would not be required in England.

It is probable that should Her Majesty's government still allow cattle to be imported from this country, a very strict supervision will be exercised over them at the ports of embarkation, and care will be taken to prevent the shipment of diseased cattle.

Mr. Evarts sent me a copy of a telegram which he forwarded on the 1st instant to Mr. Welsh, a copy of which I have the honor to inclose.

I have made inquiries of several persons in and about Washington as to the prevalence of pleuro-pneumonia among cattle in the neighborhood. I find that there are isolated cases of the disease here and there, but many less than in June last, when there were several deaths on account of it. The cases seem to be confined to milch cows, and more particularly to those kept in stables.

In the latter case the disease will attack a good many cows, but will not spread outside the stable, and seems to be due to local causes.

Dr. Fairfax, a gentleman of English descent, who has lived for many years on a farm in Maryland, nine or ten miles from here, who is thoroughly acquainted with such matters, and whose statements can be entirely relied upon, says that the disease in this country is not the same as in England; that it is not considered to be contagious, and that it has not become epidemic, although it will spread in a stable where the animals are subjected to the same local circumstances.

I have this afternoon received a telegram from the Governor-General of Canada, informing me of the Order of the Privy Council of the Dominion, prohibiting, for three months from the 1st instant, the introduction of cattle from the United States into the different provinces of the Dominion.

I have, &c.,

EDWARD THORNTON.

[Inclosure 1 in No. 2.]

Letter from Mr. Evarts to Sir Edward Thornton.

DEPARTMENT OF STATE, *Washington, January* 30, 1879.

MY DEAR SIR EDWARD : I have received information that an inspector of the British Government has been in New York and Alexandria for some days past, and has reported to the Canadian Government the existence of pleuro-pneumonia among cattle.

I presume that information to the same effect may have been communicated to you by him. I am not myself aware of the existence of the disease, but as the cattle trade between this country and Great Britain is of so great importance, and as any interruption of it is likely to have such serious results, I shall be very glad, indeed, to be informed of any intelligence which you may have received upon the subject, or to confer with you.

I am, &c.,

WM. M. EVARTS.

[Inclosure 2 in No. 2.]

Letter from Mr. Crump to Sir Edward Thornton.

BRITISH CONSULATE, PHILADELPHIA, UNITED STATES. (No date.)

I think I ought to write you with reference to the latest development in the cattle disease. You may not be aware that Prof. D. McEachran, Veterinary Inspector of Canada, who, I am told, was introduced to you in Canada, has been through some of the cities of the United States on a confidential mission inspecting cattle, particularly with reference to the existence of pleuro-pneumonia. He was in this city, Washington, and Virginia last week, and returned to Canada a few days ago, after making inspections on Long Island that resulted in painful developments. I am informed that he did not desire to visit any official of the Imperial Government, as he was not instructed to do so; that he did not call upon you while he was in Washington, and declined a pressing invitation to confer with me while in this city. He discovered in Williamsburg, near Brooklyn, a shocking state of things. There is a byre, a cow-house, connected with a distillery, where cows are housed to the number of 800 at a time, and fed with hot swill running along the troughs in front of the cattle connected with the distillery. The object to be attained is to increase the production of milk, which is obtained to an extraordinary extent. The cattle never get out of this place in a healthy condition, and but few alive, the pleuro-pneumonia killing them off, several per day, or rather they are sold for a small sum before death to Jew dealers, who kill and dress the meat for New York, to be retailed, not to Jews, but only to the Christian consumers. A few young cattle, when first infected, are returned to the country, there, in all probability, to spread the disease. The milk and meat of these animals are dangerous to the human system. They are not allowed to be sold in Brooklyn, but can be passed through that city to New York. The temperature of the numerous cases of pleuro-pneumonia examined by Dr. McEachran was as high as 105°, and in some cases 107^C, showing the most virulent type of the complaint. The animals get no exercise whatever, leaving their stalls, to which they are chained, for slaughter when attacked by the contagion. The filth, heat, and fetid steam of the place, it is reported, are of the most revolting character. Dr. McEachran's entrance into this place was clandestine, and, upon being discovered, he narrowly escaped personal violence. I have requested my informant, a veterinary surgeon of this city, of ability, and the highest character in the city, Dr. Gadsden, to write me a letter. He has done so, and I beg to forward it to you.

I should also state that Dr. McEachran found much pleuro-pneumonia in Alexandria, Va., where two or three hundred cases terminated fatally last year. He says the complaint extends all over the State of Virginia. Dr. McEachran has returned to Canada with a determination to have steps taken for the protection of the Canadian stock-yards from this infection and the stigma that will follow the disclosure of these facts.

To-day cable news has been received in this city that a cargo of live cattle from Portland had been found afflicted with pleuro-pneumonia on arrival at Liverpool, and the animals were all killed. This news came to Eastman, of New York, the largest shipper in the country, and who is said to be carrying out the plans of Vanderbilt and the New York Central Railway. Other cable news has been received that steps are about to be taken to forbid the landing of cattle from American ports. Samuel Allerton & Co., of Chicago, the largest shippers of dead meat, and from this port, as well as others engaged in this fast-becoming most important trade, are much exercised.

A certificate of inspection of a cargo of live cattle per steamship Lord Clive, sailed to-day from Philadelphia to Liverpool, was presented to me for authentication, but as I did not know the character of the inspector I declined to certify to it. Subsequently, however, when it was returned attested by the collector of the port, that the inspector was appointed by him to perform the duty, I certified to the official act of the collector.

The merchants here engaged in the trade are willing to adopt any plan that I may suggest to them, regardless of the expense, to insure the shipment of healthy animals and meat to England.

Dr. McEachran made no discoveries in this district unfavorable to the general healthy condition of the cattle.

P. S.—Dr. McEachran had a long interview with the Commissioner of Agriculture in your city. I believe he did not visit Boston. Large numbers of live cattle are shipped from Boston in the winter, which come originally from Canada, and are on Canadian account.

[Inclosure 3, No. 2.]

Letter from Mr Gadsden, M. R. C. V. S., to George Crump, Esq.

134 NORTH TENTH STREET, PHILADELPHIA, *January 28*, 1879.

Knowing you wish all the information respecting contagious diseases of cattle, I send you a report of my examination of some with Prof. D. McEachran, the Veterinary Inspector of Canada, who was sent by his government to investigate it and report at once.

The Inspector called on me first on his way to Washington (18th instant); again on the 23d of this month, when he reported to me he had examined several cases of contagious pleuro-pneumonia in cattle at Alexandria, Va.

I started with him on the 24th to New York to find out the truth of the report that a contagious disease was prevalent on Long Island. We found very many cases of contagious pleuro-pneumonia in a large byre, or cow-house, containing about 800 cows (all in a filthy condition), at Williamsburg,* near Brooklyn. This large cow-house adjoins the distillery of Gaff, Fleischman & Co., where they are fed on hot swill and hay, to force the milk. This place is a regular pest-house for the disease; the cows belong to a large number of milkmen, who pay a small sum (77 cents per cow a week) for the stall and swill. It is quite impossible for me to inform you how many of these 800 cows have the disease at the present time, but I should think from what I saw that several hundred have it now, and it is only a question of time for all the others to take it. The men would not allow us to examine many of them in one part; we found very few healthy cows there. We made a *post-mortem* examination of the lungs of one of the cows that had this disease in the last stage, which leaves no doubt of its character, as all the pathological anatomy of this malady was present (one lung was very heavy and quite solid). Just before the cows die they are killed and sent into New York market as good beef (at night).

From inquiry made by us from cattlemen and veterinary surgeons at Brooklyn, we have no doubt that this disease is prevalent in many parts of Long Island, as these diseased cows from Williamsburg are often sent away alive to other parts of the island.

I have made inquiry from several veterinary-surgeons in Pennsylvania, but cannot hear of any contagious diseases in cattle in the State.

[Inclosure 4 in No. 2.]

Telegram from Mr. Evarts to Mr. Welsh, United States Minister, London.

FEBRUARY, 1, 1879.

Cattle by Ontario, part Canadian, part Western. Inspection offered by government was declined by shippers on their view that British regulations did not require it. There is no evidence of any disease in the cattle of this country that affects domestic or foreign trade in them. This government would regard our proscription of our trade in live cattle as wholly unjustified by any condition of things known or suspected here. The appearance of pleuro-pneumonia in a cargo at the end of a voyage can scarcely warrant a restriction of this trade with a country free from any epidemic among cattle. Communicate to Salisbury.

No. 3.

Letter from the United States Minister, London, to the Marquis of Salisbury.

LEGATION OF THE UNITED STATES, *London, February* 4, 1879.

MY LORD: The arrival of the Dominion steamer "Ontario" from Portland last week at Liverpool, with a number of cattle, a few of which were said to have had the pleuro-pneumonia, has been the occasion of much anxiety to those who have recently embarked very largely in the importation of cattle from the United States.

It has been asserted in the newspapers that these cattle were brought from Chicago and Buffalo, in the United States, and further, that an expert, having been employed by the Canadian authorities for the purpose, had visited the United States and found in Washington and elsewhere some cattle affected by the disease.

These circumstances have caused me to make such inquiries as were essential to an understanding of the facts of the case, the results of which I beg to place before your Lordship.

From reliable parties in Liverpool I learn that while a part of the cattle by the Ontario came from Chicago and a part from Buffalo, at least 45 head of them came from Toronto, and were so mixed with the others that the Canadian and the United States cattle could not be distinguished. It is also beyond dispute that those which came from the United States passed for several hundred miles over the Grand Trunk road through the Dominion of Canada; that all the cattle were exposed to weather of unusual severity; that they remained for a considerable time in Portland without food or water; and that they had undergone an exceptional amount of hardship and bad usage before entering upon a voyage which was made at an inclement season and during excessively rough weather. Under these circumstances it is strange that so few

* Blissville is no doubt meant.

were found whose lungs were diseased. In fact, the fact that so few were found diseased is almost a conclusive proof that they were healthy when they left their several places of departure, for had they been then affected by a contagious or infectious malady, as the pleuro-pneumonia is asserted to be, would it not have been communicated to most, if not to all, of the herd?

What I have just narrated is the result of my inquiry on this side. So soon as the report reached me I telegraphed to the Department of State at Washington for the facts, both in regard to this special case and to the existence of pleuro-pneumonia among the cattle in the United States. Mr. Evarts replied as follows:

"Cattle by Ontario, part Canadian, part Western. Inspection offered by government was declined by shippers on their view that British regulations did not require it. There is no evidence of any disease in the cattle of this country that affects domestic or foreign trade in them.

"This government would regard any proscription of our trade in live cattle as wholly unjustified by any condition of things known or suspected here. The appearance of pleuro-pneumonia in the cargo at the end of a voyage can scarcely warrant a restriction of this trade with a country free from any epidemic among cattle."

The accounts from both sides, so far as this cargo is concerned, seem to me not to warrant the inference that the pleuro-pneumonia exists either in Canada or the United States; but if the few cattle which were diseased really had it, the hardships and exposure which they underwent are sufficient to account for it.

Your lordship should not lose sight of the fact that our laws exclude the importation of all cattle from Europe into the United States on account of the fear of disease, unless under the special permission of the Secretary of State, and then only of such kinds as are needed for breeding purposes.

Since the arrival of the Ontario several vessels have reached here from the United States with cattle which were entirely healthy.

I trust it will prove that the alarm which has arisen from this single case has been quite unnecessary, and that nothing further will occur to check the development of a trade which promises such large employment for the tonnage of Great Britain, and an advantageous market for the abundant herds of America. I am quite sure, however, that in no event will your lordship allow of hasty and inconsiderate action unfavorable to the interests of the United States.

It will come to the knowledge of your lordship from authoritative sources that the representatives of about one-third of the entire steam tonnage of the United Kingdom, the Ship-owners' Association of Liverpool, believe that the true interests of the people of Great Britain are to be promoted, not by a greater restriction in existing rules, but by their enlargement, so that the cattle coming from North America shall be subject to the same regulations which control cattle coming from Ireland, and from one port in the Kingdom to another.

I have, &c.,

JOHN WELSH.

No. 4.

Letter from the United States Minister, London, to the Marquis of Salisbury.

LEGATION OF UNITED STATES OF AMERICA, *London, February 7, 1879.*

MY LORD: Since I wrote you on the subject of the transit of cattle from America, and the alarm which the few cases of disease on the Ontario had occasioned, the following vessels, viz., the Victoria, England, State of Alabama, Illyrian, Pembroke, and Iberian, have arrived at Liverpool, and discharged their several parcels of cattle without a single case of disease all having passed after a most critical inspection. Notwithstanding this, rumors exist in Liverpool that the privy council will, at an early day, put the United States on the schedule, and subject all cattle coming thence to slaughter on arrival. This has created the greatest alarm, because of the large interests involved, and, as it is claimed, of the great injustice to which the parties will be subjected without any adequate notice.

The freedom from disease in the cattle from the United States which have hitherto been brought to England, and among recent arrivals, seem to me to forbid any action which would be so serious in its consequences, or even any interruption in the trade now existing, and I shall be glad to be authorized by you to say that the present apprehensions are unfounded.

I have, &c.,

JOHN WELSH.

No. 5.

Letter from the Clerk of the Council to the Under Secretary of State, Foreign Office.

VETERINARY DEPARTMENT, PRIVY COUNCIL OFFICE,
44 PARLIAMENT STREET, WESTMINSTER, S. W., *February* 12, 1879.

SIR: I have submitted to the lords of the council your letter of the 8th instant, inclosing copies of two notes from the United States Minister respecting the cases of pleuro-pneumonia recently detected at Liverpool among cattle, ex Ontario, from the United States, and deprecating any increase of the restrictions in the cattle trade with America.

In reply, I am directed to state, for the information of Lord Salisbury, that in consequence of the reports which have reached the Lords of the Council of the existence of pleuro-pneumonia in the United States of America, coupled with the fact that animals affected with that disease have been landed at Liverpool, their lordships have no option under the terms of the contagious diseases (animals) act, 1878, but to revoke that portion of the Order of Council by which the United States were exempted from the the provisions of that act.

I beg to inclose a copy of the Order of Council which the Lords of the Council have considered it necessary to pass, and which comes into operation on the 4th proximo.

I am, &c.,

C. L. PEEL.

———

[Inclosure in No. 5.]

At the Council Chamber, 467 Whitehall, the 10th of February, 1879.
By the Lords of Her Majesty's Most Honorable Privy Council.
Present: Lord President, Lord John Manners.

The Lords and others of Her Majesty's Most Honorable Privy Council, by virtue and in exercise of the powers in them vested under the contagious diseases (animals) act 1878 (in this order referred to as the act of 1878) and of every other power enabling them in this behalf, do order, and it is hereby ordered, as follows:

1. This Order shall take effect from and immediately after the 3d day of March, 1879, and words in this order have the same meaning as in the act of 1878.
2. This Order extends to Great Britain only.
3. Article 13 of the Foreign Animals Order is hereby revoked, as far as it relates to cattle brought from the United States of America, and declares that the same may be landed without being subject under the act of 1878, or under that Order, to slaughter or to quarantine.

C. L. PEEL.

———

[No. 6.]

Letter from the British Consul-General at New York to the Marquis of Salisbury.

BRITISH CONSULATE GENERAL, *New York, January* 30, 1879.

MY LORD: I have the honor to report to your lordship that in order to obtain the latest and most authentic information in regard to the sanitary condition of animals in this consular district, I addressed on the 24th instant a circular letter to the secretaries of the respective State governments of New York, New Jersey, Connecticut, Delaware, and Rhode Island, in this consular district, calling attention to the statements of a professor of veterinary science that cases of pleuro-pneumonia are not infrequent in these States, and requesting to be furnished with any information in their possession on this subject; requesting also that my communication might be referred to the State agricultural department or society, and asking that the desired information should be furnished to me as speedily as possible.

In case of the known existence of any cases, requesting further that, with regard to the nature of the disease, it might be stated whether or not it is regarded as contagious, had become epidemic, to what extent it had proved fatal, the treatment adopted for its cure, and what, if any, provision had been made for arresting its extension.

I received from the secretary of state of the State of New York a reply, of which I inclose a copy, informing me that that department has no knowledge relative to pleuro-pneumonia existing among animals in this State. From the secretary of the State agricultural society, with whom I also communicated, I received replies, of which I inclose extracts, from which it will be seen that he questions the existence of contagious pleuro-pneumonia in this country.

I inclose also copies of the last annual report of the society, recently adopted, in which, while reference is made to the act of the legislature of last year respecting infectious and contagious diseases of animals (copies of which I transmitted to Her Majesty's legation at Washington in September last), no allusion whatever is made to the existence of contagious diseases among live stock in this State.

From the State of Connecticut, however, I have received a letter from Mr. T. S. Gold, one of the commissioners on diseases of domestic animals, of which I inclose a copy, reporting the outbreak of contagious pleuro-pneumonia in one herd of cows in the town of Watertown, in that State. He adds that the disease is not epidemic, but is confined to this one herd, which is strictly quarantined; that the commissioners know of no other cases in the State, and are quite sure that none others exist.

In regard to the State of New Jersey, I have received from a member of the State board of health a letter, of which I inclose a copy, informing me that he has recently investigated the sanitary condition of live stock in that State, and finds that contagious pleuro-pneumonia has existed, and at the present time does exist, to a more or less degree. That so far as he can learn it has never assumed the epizootic form. That at the present time it is found in isolated cases, which might be the means of superinducing an outbreak.

From the States of Delaware and Rhode Island I have as yet received no replies to my inquiries.

On receipt of the communication from Connecticut and the statement therein of the supposition that the disease had been imported from New York in August last, and upon a report made to me that pleuro-pneumonia among cows was supposed to lurk in some of the dairies in the suburbs of New York and Brooklyn, more especially in dairies in connection with large breweries, I addressed a letter to the respective mayors of the two cities, calling their attention to the matter, and requesting that an investigation might be made, and that I might be informed of the result.

I think it well to inclose a copy of a letter from the agricultural editor of the American Agriculturist, supposed to be well informed in such matters, stating that among grazing cattle there is now no disease reported in any part of the country; that occasionally a few cases of pneumonia occur in ill-conducted dairies, but that it is not of an epizootic character, and remains in the States where it originated. He concludes by stating that there now is none of this existing, a conclusion, however, which is at variance with the positive reports from Connecticut and New Jersey.

I have to-day seen and conversed with Mr. Eastman, who is the principal shipper of fresh meat from this port, and who in the summer time has exported live stock from hence to Great Britain. He largely supplies this market, and handles about 2,500 head of cattle every week. He assures me that in the Western States, from whence he draws his supplies, there are absolutely no diseases—certainly no contagious diseases—among cattle.

In pursuance of the information which I had received, I yesterday transmitted to your lordship the following telegram :

" A few isolated cases of pleuro-pneumonia among horned cattle have appeared within this consular district. Fuller report by post."

E. M. ARCHIBALD.

[Inclosure 1 in No. 6.]

Letter from Mr. Allen C. Beach to E. M. Archibald, Esq., Her Britannic Majesty's Consul-General, New York.

STATE OF NEW YORK, OFFICE OF THE SECRETARYOF STATE,
Albany, January 28, 1879.

In answer to your favor of the 24th instant, I have the honor to state that this department has no knowledge relative to pleuro-pneumonia existing among animals in this State.

I have applied to the secretary of the State agricultural society, who I thought would be most likely to give you the information desired, and am informed that he has written you in full upon the subject.

[Inclosure 2, in No. 6.]

Letter from Secretary New York Agricultural Society to E. M. Archibald, Esq., Her Britannic Majesty's Consul-General, New York.

JANUARY 24, 1879.

I am in receipt of your letter of yesterday, and have much pleasure in sending a copy of the report made by the executive committee to the general meeting of the

S. Ex. 5——3

society on Wednesday last. The society's report to the legislature has not yet been presented.

I am not in possession of any other information on the subject of the disease among cows near Washington other than that given in the New York Tribune, and I very much distrust the diagnosis given in that paper, and based upon report only. It would seem that had the disease been the contagious lung plague (pleuro-pneumonia) of Europe, we should have heard of larger losses and of continued mortality.

We have never been called upon to investigate a case of pleuro-pneumonia. We have frequently had to send to investigate mysterious outbreaks of disease reported in the newspapers, but they have invariably turned out to be splenic apoplexy (anthrax). The only diseases of cattle that have ever occurred as epidemics in our cattle markets are Texan fever and the foot-and-mouth disease. The former has given no cause for alarm since 1868, except locally, and in one town and on only one farm in 1877, where it disappeared almost before we had time to be sure of its identity. The latter did not survive the first winter after its importation, and if it occurs again it will be from a new importation.

As to pleuro-pneumonia, which in one form is of course contagious (and probably the hardest of all diseases to get rid of), opinions differ as to whether it exists in this country or not. Professor Law, in the paper which he read at our annual meeting in 1876 (see our Transactions, volume xxxii), probably puts the case for the affirmative as strongly as possible. On the other hand, there is the fact that we hear of no cases in recent years of disease supposed to be pleuro-pneumonia, or pronounced to be by any competent authority. The last report of it that I know of was by Professor Cressy to the Connecticut Board of Agriculture, in 1874, and in that case the identification of the disease with the contagious pleuro-pneumonia of Europe seems to be doubtful, because the animals were purchased in the autumn and remained sound until the spring; whereas three months is the longest period of incubation claimed for the disease by Professor Law and two months by Gamgee (Domestic Animals in Health and Disease, vol. 1, page 602). I am, therefore, inclined to believe the Connecticut disease to have been the sporadic pleuro-pneumonia described by Gamgee (in the work cited) rather than the contagious form. It seems hard to believe that so fatal a disease should be lurking, as some maintain that it is, among the dairies of the lower class in the neighborhood of our large Atlantic cities without spreading and without causing such loss as to attract attention; but if such be the fact, the situation of our important cattle markets and the way in which the movement of cattle is carried on render it almost impossible that the disease can become epidemic.

[Inclosure 3 in No. 6.]

Letter from Secretary New York Agricultural Society to E. M. Archibald, Esq., Her Britannic Majesty's Consul-General, New York.

JANUARY, 25, 1879.

In reply to your note of yesterday, I have to say that if it was Professor Law who wrote the article in the Tribune of 27th of November, it accounts for the very decided tone in which the Washington disease was pronounced to be contagious pleuro-pneumonia.

As to the disease which under the name of pleuro-pneumonia has occurred, or has been reported occasionally of late years in the United States, being identical with the contagious pleuro-pneumonia of Europe I very much doubt for the reasons given in my letter of yesterday.

It is generally admitted, and supposed to be established, that the disease imported in Mr. Chenery's Holland cattle at Boston in 1859, and in Mr. Richardson's shorthorns in 1847, was contagious pleuro-pneumonia. In both these cases the disease is believed to have been extirpated.

The foundation for the statement that the same disease came to this country in 1843 and in 1850 I do not know. Writing in 1860 on the subject of the disease then prevailing in Massachusetts, the late Mr. B. P. Johnson, the secretary of this society, used the following language:

" At the same time it may be proper to note that, according to evidence too full and well authenticated to be rejected, pleuro-pneumonia has in several instances made its appearance in this country previous to its introduction by Mr. Chenery's importations. Cases in past years in the vicinity of several of our cities, of its attacks, and subsequent entire extirpation, have been brought to our notice in detail," &c.—(Transactions New York State Ag. Soc., 1859, p. 783.)

I think it may properly be inferred from this language that in 1859 we supposed the country to be free from pleuro-pneumonia of the contagious form, and we know that the authorities of Massachusetts considered that in 1861 they had completely rid that State of the contagion imported in 1859. I am not in a position to assert that there has been no later importation. I can only say that I have never heard of any.

[Inclosure 4 in No. 6.]

Letter from T. S. Gold, Esq., to E. M. Archibald, Esq., Her Britannic Majesty's Consul-General, New York.

JANUARY 29, 1879.

Yours of 24th instant has been referred to me by the Honorary Secretary of State, and in reply would say that one herd of cows in Watertown is suffering at present with pleuro-pneumonia. Of 19 head, four have died, one sick cow has been killed, and most of the others are affected. It is plainly contagious, and we attribute the disease to two cows brought from New York in August. It is not epidemic, but is confined to this one herd, which is strictly quarantined. We know of no other cases in this State, and we are quite sure that none exist.

One or two similar outbreaks have been controlled by slaughter and quarantine.

Dr. Noah Cressy, V. S., is treating this herd, principally relying upon alcoholic stimulants, but it is too early to speak of results.

[Inclosure 5 in No. 6.]

Letter from Henry C. Kelsey, Esq., to E. M. Archibald, Esq., Her Britannic Majesty's Consul-General, New York.

JANUARY 9, 1879.

Your favor of the 24th instant is this day referred to William M. Force, Esq., Newark, N. J., Secretary of the State Agricultural Society, for answer.

[Inclosure 6 in No. 6.]

Letter from Mr. J. C. Corlies, D. V. S., to E. M. Archibald, Esq., Her Britannic Majesty's Consul-General, New York.

NEWARK, NEW JERSEY, *January 28, 1879.*

My esteemed friend, Mr. W. M. Force, has requested me to answer a communication conveyed to him through the State Department from yourself in reference to pleuro-pneumonia as existing in the Atlantic coast States. I have the honor to say that, as a member of the State board of health, it has recently been my duty to look into and investigate the sanitary condition of the live stock of our State (New Jersey), and in so doing I find that pleuro-pneumonia has and does exist to a more or less degree at the present time; and, so far as we can learn, it has never assumed the epizootic form, while on several occasions it may be said to have presented an enzootic form. But, usually, and at the present time, it is found in isolated cases, which may be the means of at any time superinducing an outbreak.

It is always of a contagious character, and entails a mortality of about fifty per cent. of the affected cases, &c., &c.

The preventive measures consist of quarantining, inoculation, and, in radical cases, occision. There have been three special acts enacted by the State legislature for the purpose of arresting its progress on the appearance of an outbreak, the substance of which is conferring power upon township authorities to employ competent medical advice, and, if it should be found necessary, to resort to occision, and the owner to be compensated by the State.

[Inclosure 7 in No. 6.]

Letter from the Editor of the American Agriculturist to E. M. Archibald, Esq., Her Britannic Majesty's Consul-General, New York.

JANUARY 21, 1879.

Your inquiry about diseases of cattle has been referred to me. In reply I beg to say that I know of no disease that is now prevalent among cattle in any part of the country. We have occasionally a few scattered cases of pneumonia occurring in ill-conducted dairies, but it is not of an epizootic character and remains in the stables where it originated. Amongst grazing cattle there is now no disease reported in any part of the country. Our climate fortunately forbids the occurrence of those diseases which prevail in some European countries, and past experience has shown that the cases of pleuro-pneumonia which have occurred at times a few years ago were neither virulent nor difficult to deal with, and that ordinary sanitary precautions now practiced are sufficient to keep it in check. Just now there is none of this existing.

No. 7.

Telegram from Consul-General Archibald to the Marquis of Salisbury.

FEBRUARY 8, 1879.

The cattle disease near Brooklyn, Long Island, is decidedly contagious; pleuro-pneumonia extensively prevalent. There is possibility of contagion affecting Western cattle shipped from this port.

No. 8.

Telegram from Consul-General Archibald to the Marquis of Salisbury.

FEBRUARY 9, 1878.

My telegram yesterday meant extensively prevalent in a large stable near Brooklyn, in which are about 800 cows, and from whence diseased cows are said to have been sent to other parts of Long Island.

No. 9.

Telegram from Foreign Office to Consul-General Archibald.

FEBRUARY 12, 3.50 p. m.

Reference to your telegram of 8th instant. Report by telegram name and owner of stable and address where disease is situated; also the veterinary evidence that it is contagious pleuro-pneumonia. Write full particulars by next post.

No. 10.

Letter from Consul-General Archibald to the Marquis of Salisbury.

JANUARY 30, 1879.

MY LORD: With reference to my dispatch (No. 8) of 21st instant, I have the honor to transmit herewith inclosed, for your Lordship's information, copy of a dispatch, and of its inclosures, received by me from Sir Edward Thornton, communicating the report of an investigation made by the health officer of the District of Columbia, in regard to the real nature of the disease reported to exist among cows in the vicinity of Washington, and referred to in the inclosure of your Lordship's dispatch No. 1, of the 2d instant, from which report it appears that the disease is pleuro-pneumonia.

The author of the observations in the Tribune newspaper, of the 27th November last, on the reported "plague" at Washington, is Dr. James Law, professor of veterinary science in the Cornell University, at Ithaca, in this State, and one whose opinions are well deserving of consideration.

I have not as yet received from the president of the New York College of Veterinary Surgeons his promised report upon this subject.

Referring your Lordship for further information to my dispatch (Consular No. 10) of this date,

I have, &c.,

E. M. ARCHIBALD.

[Inclosure 1 in No. 10.]

Letter from Sir Edward Thornton to E. M. Archibald, Esq., Her Britannic Majesty's Consul-General, New York.

WASHINGTON, *January* 30, 1879.

I have the honor to transmit herewith copy of a note, and of its inclosures, which I have received from Mr. Evarts, from which you will perceive that it is admitted that there have been cases of pleuro-pneumonia, or lung fever, among the cows in the neighborhood of Washington. As it would appear from the Order in Council of the 6th ultimo that the above-mentioned disease is considered to be contagious, I have addressed a further note to Mr. Evarts, inquiring as to the extent of the disease and what steps have been taken to prevent its spreading.

[Inclosure 2 in No. 10.]

Letter from Mr. Evarts to Sir Edward Thornton.

DEPARTMENT OF STATE,
Washington, January 27, 1879.

SIR: I have the honor to acknowledge the receipt of Mr. Drummond's note of the 16th instant, in which, on behalf of Her Majesty's Government, inquiry is made in reference to the existence among the cows in the vicinity of Washington of a disease similar to the rinderpest, and also as to whether any such or other form of disease has lately prevailed among the cows in or about this city.

In reply, I have to state that the matter has been referred to the Board of Commissioners of the District of Columbia, and that a reply thereto has been received from the president of that body, dated the 24th instant, accompanied by a report on the subject from the health officer of the District, copies of both of which are herewith inclosed for your information.

I have, &c.,

WM. M. EVARTS.

[Inclosure 3 in No. 10.]

Letter from President of the Commissioners, District of Columbia, to Hon. W. M. Evarts, inclosing a report from the Medical Officer of Health.

OFFICE OF THE COMMISSIONERS OF THE DISTRICT OF COLUMBIA,
Washington, January 24, 1879.

SIR: In response to your request of the 22d instant, that the Commissioners take measures to ascertain whether the rinderpest or any other form of disease has lately prevailed among the cows in or about the city of Washington, the Commissioners have the honor to say that they referred the matter to the health officer of the District immediately upon the receipt of your communication for investigation, and herewith submit a copy of his report in the premises.

By order of the board.

S. L. PHELPS, *President.*

[Inclosure 4 in No. 10.]

OFFICE OF HEALTH OFFICER, *January 24,* 1879.

Respectfully returned to the Commissioners, District of Columbia, with the following information :

About the 17th of October, 1878, a gentleman residing in the county of Washington, near this city, called at this office and requested the examination of some cattle then ill on his farm. An inspector having considerable experience with disease of cattle was sent ; he made careful and thorough examination of the animals on this and adjoining farms, and reported them suffering from pleuro-pneumonia, or lung fever.

A morning paper in this city made a sensational report of this matter, heading the same "Rinderpest," and from this probably sprung the reports which are said to have appeared in certain New York papers. I have been called upon several times to deny the story, and would again state that careful inspection of the dairy farms in this vicinity has failed to reveal the existence of any disease similar to the rinderpest or cattle-plague.

SMITH TOWNSHEND, M. D., *Health Officer.*

Official copy :

WILLIAM TINDALL, *Secretary.*

No.. 11.

Letter from United States Minister, London, to the Marquis of Salisbury.

LEGATION OF THE UNITED STATES, LONDON, *February 19,* 1879.

MY LORD: I have the honor to acquaint you that I have just received from Mr. Evarts a circular, of which I inclose copy, and which has been addressed by the Secretary of the Treasury of the United States to collectors of customs and others.

Your lordship will observe that by this document collectors of customs are instructed not to permit shipments of live animals from their respective ports until after an inspection of such animals with reference to their freedom from disease, and the issuance of a certificate showing that they are free from the class of maladies mentioned.

I beg to express the hope that these precautionary measures may have some influence in inducing Her Majesty's Privy Council to rescind or modify their order in relation to this matter of the 10th instant.

I have, &c.,

JOHN WELSH.

[Inclosure in No. 11.]

Copy of a circular in relation to cattle disease, issued by the Secretary of the Treasury, February 1, 1879.

[Circular.]

INFORMATION IN REGARD TO CATTLE DISEASE.

TREASURY DEPARTMENT,
Washington, D. C., February 1, 1879.

By department's circular of December 18, 1878, it was directed that live cattle shipped from the various ports of the United States might be examined with reference to the question whether they were free from contagious diseases, and that if found to be free from such diseases a certificate to that effect should be given. By that circular such inspection was not made compulsory, but the certificate was to be issued only upon the application of parties interested.

As the export trade in live cattle from the United States is of vital importance to large interests, every precaution should be taken to guard against the shipment of diseased animals abroad, and such a guarantee given as will satisfy foreign countries, especially Great Britain, that no risk will ensue from such shipments of communicating contagious or infectious diseases to the animals in foreign countries by shipments from the United States.

Collectors of customs are therefore instructed that in no case will live animals be permitted to be shipped from their respective ports until after an inspection of the animals with reference to their freedom from disease, and the issuance of a certificate showing that they are free from the class of diseases mentioned.

Notice of rejected cattle should be promptly given to this department.

In order that this department may be fully informed in regard to such diseases in any part of the United States, collectors of customs are requested to promptly forward to this department any information which they may be able to obtain of the presence of contagious or infectious diseases prevailing among live animals in their vicinity.

It is probable that if the disease prevails to any considerable extent it will be noticed in the local press, and collectors are requested to send copies of any notices to the department for its information.

JOHN SHERMAN, *Secretary.*

To COLLECTORS OF CUSTOMS AND OTHERS.

No. 12.

Letter from the Clerk of the Council to the Under Secretary of State, Foreign Office.

VETERINARY DEPARTMENT, PRIVY COUNCIL OFFICE,
44 *Parliament Street, Westminster, S. W., February* 27, 1879.

SIR: I have submitted to the Lords of the Council your letter of the 22d instant transmitting a dispatch, with inclosure, from the United States Minister at this court on the subject of the export of cattle from the United States of America to Great Britain.

In reply I am directed to state for the information of Lord Salisbury that the Lords of the Council have carefully considered the orders given by the American Government for the inspection of cattle previous to exportation. Their lordships are, however, aware from their own experience that no system of inspection at the port, however perfect, affords complete security against the introduction of pleuro-pneumonia. So long, therefore, as that disease exists in the United States, their Lordships regret that, looking to the provisions of the contagious diseases animals act, 1878, relative to importation of foreign animals, they are unable to modify the Order of the 10th of February, 1870, which prohibits the introduction into Great Bri tain, except for slaugh-ter, of cattle from the United States of America.

I beg to return the dispatch and inclosure as requested.

I am, &c.,

C. L. PEEL.

No. 13.

Extract from a message from the President of the United States, communicating, in answer to a Senate resolution of 20th February, 1878, information in relation to the disease pre-vailing among swine and other domestic animals.

EXECUTIVE MANSION, *February* 27, 1878.

To the Senate of the United States :

I transmit herewith, for the information of the Senate, the reply of the Commis-sioner of Agriculture to a resolution of the Senate of the 20th instant, "relative to the disease prevailing among swine," &c.

R. B. HAYES.

DEPARTMENT OF AGRICULTURE,
Washington, D. C., February 26th, 1878.

SIR: In compliance with a resolution of the Senate, adopted on the 20th instant, calling upon me for such information as may be in my possession relative to the disease prvailing among swine commonly known as "hog cholera," with such suggestions as I may deem pertinent in this connection, I have the honor to herewith transmit a large number of letters from almost every section of the country relating to this and the many diseases to which all other classes of domestic animals are subject. For some years past the local press, and especially the agricultural journals of the country, have been calling attention to the increase of diseases among farm stock, and the consequent heavy losses annually sustained by our farmers and stock breeders and growers.

Our wide extent of country, and its great diversity of temperature and variation of cli-mate, the severity of frosts in some sections, and the intensity of heat in other local-ities, render farm stock liable to the attacks and ravages of almost everye disease known in the history of domestic animals.   So general and fatal have many of these mala-dies grown, that stock breeding and rearing has to some extent become a precarious call-ing, instead of the profitable business of former years.   This would seem to be espe-cially true as it relates to swine.   Year by year new diseases, heretofore unknown in our country, make their appearance among this class of farm animals, while older ones become permanently localized, and much more fatal in their results.   Farmers, as a general thing, are neglectful of their stock, and pay but little attention to sporadic cases of sickness among their flocks and herds.   It is only when diseases become gen-eral, and consequently of an epidemic and contagious character, that active measures are taken for the relief of the animals afflicted.   It is then generally too late, as reme-dies have ceased to have their usual beneficial effects, and the disease is only stayed when it has no more victims to prey upon.

BRONCHITIS.

Prof. W. Williams, of the New Veterinary College of Edinburgh, Scotland, has, during the past few years, paid much attention to the study of diseases affecting the air-passages and lungs of domesticated animals. In the second edition of his work, which seems to have been revised with great care, he treats at considerable length of the diseases known as pleuro-pneumonia contagiosa and bronchitis in horned cattle, and points out with distinctness the difference between those diseases. His conclusions are of great importance in the present controversy. In the preface to the second edition of his work, Professor Williams says:

"The existence and characteristics of pleuro-pneumonia contagiosa and bronchitis in horned cattle were lately the subject of differences of opinion between the veterinary officers of the privy council and the author, in connection with the alleged existence of pleuro among American cattle imported into this country, and slaughtered at Liverpool to prevent contagion. The author has very carefully studied the post-mortem appearances of both diseases, and submits his conclusions to the profession. The opportunity of studying the *post-mortem* appearances of bronchitis in its earlier stages but seldom occurs; and had it not been for the slaughter of the cattle referred to the lesions induced by the initial stages of inflammation of the bronchial tubes could not have been so minutely demonstrated.

"The author does not deny the existence of pleuro in some of the Eastern States of America, but it has not yet been proved that this contagious malady prevails in the Western States, from whence cattle are brought to this country. Of this, however, he is confident, that in none of the diseased lungs of the cattle referred to did he find the characteristics of contagious pleuro; but, in all, those of bronchitis. In this investigation he has received much valuable assistance from Dr. Hamilton, pathologist to the Royal Infirmary, and demonstrator of morbid anatomy in the University of Edinburgh."

BRONCHITIS.

The following is the full text of Professor Williams' article on this subject:

Division.—This disease may, according to its seat, be arranged under four heads, namely, "tracheo-bronchitis," where the lower part of the trachea and larger tubes are the main seat of the inflammation; "bronchitis proper," where the medium-sized bronchi are the chief seats of the disease; "capillary bronchitis," where the smaller bronchi are chiefly implicated; and "catarrhal, lobular, or broncho pneumonia," where the smallest bronchi and alveolar walls are involved in the inflammatory process. For simplicity of description I shall retain the generic term bronchitis, dividing it into acute and chronic.

The character of the inflammation, whatever part of the respiratory tract may be affected, is what is understood as catarrhal—that is, an inflammation in which, instead of an exudation rich in fibrin, there is a fluid secretion containing a large quantity of mucus and cellular elements. In this particular it differs most essentially from inflammation of the lungs, originating in the parenchyma, and from pleuro-pneumonia, in which the pleural surface, as well as the lung structure, is involved. The exudate in these is termed "croupous" or fibrinous.

Causes.—Bronchitis, wherever its seat, is generally due to exposure to cold; it may supervene on an attack of ordinary catarrh, particularly if the animal be neglected, exposed to wet and cold, or kept in ill-ventilated stables. It may also arise without any premonitory catarrhal symptoms in both horses and cattle during voyages by sea, particularly if the weather be rough and stormy, and the animals battened down. During 1877 the author had the opportunity of seeing bronchitis in its purest form, and which proved fatal to many amongst our foreign horses imported at Leith. An instructive fact in connection with these cases was that it appeared only after rough and stormy passages; when the weather was fine no cases were observed.

Among cattle shipped to this country from America during the earlier and spring months of 1879, bronchitis was observed almost identical with that seen among the foreign horses already alluded to; as the season advanced, and the weather became warm and less stormy, the disease disappeared.

Bronchitis, like laryngitis, may be caused by the inhalation of irritant matters, and by the accidental entrance of foreign materials, as medicines or food, into the bronchial tubes. Inflammation of the bronchial tubes arising from the latter cause usually occurs in horned cattle, often as a sequel to parturient apoplexy, in which affection the power of deglutition is in a great measure lost, and where the sensibility of the glottis is, during the comatose stage, greatly diminished or entirely absent. In such cases fluid medicines incautiously administered enter the trachea and bronchi, and these may cause immediate death by suffocation, or, if not immediately fatal, induce a severe and perhaps fatal inflammation.

Again, during the state of coma, semi-fluid ingesta are apt to flow into the mouth through the flaccid œsophagus, particularly if the cow lies with its head and anterior extremities lower than the posterior ones. In parturient fever there is also very often during the earlier stages some extent of antiperistaltic action of the œsophagus, with eructations of gases from the rumen; along with such gases semi-fluid ingesta gain entrance into the fauces, and, owing to the paralyzed state of the glottis, fall into the larynx and trachea.

Catarrh or bronchitis, from other than mechanical causes, may, particularly in cattle, if the accompanying cough be long and powerful, cause some degree of vomition. The food thus vomited, or, in other words, coughed up, sometimes gains entrance into the trachea and causes a fatal issue.

Along with Mr. Borthwick, Kirkiston, I saw cases of this kind in a herd of Irish cattle brought to Scotland, and which were suffering from bronchitis and gastric irritation from neglect and exposure. Four of the herd became much worse than the rest, one died, and the other three were slaughtered. In all of them the bronchial tubes were filled with ingesta, ejected into the fauces during violent fits of coughing. Again, in several specimens of the lungs of American cattle slaughtered at Liverpool, supposed to be affected with pleuro-pneumonia, food was found in the bronchi. Is it not possible that during a rough voyage cattle may suffer to some extent from sea-sickness, and even vomition, and that the vomited matters may gain access into the trachea and bronchi? In others of the condemned American cattle the irritation was associated with the presence of filaria in the bronchi. Both the ingesta and the parasites were present only in a minority of the diseased lungs examined, and could therefore be only looked upon as accidental concomitants.

Food sometimes gains access into the trachea in the course of dissolution, or even after death, particularly if the rumen be rather full of moist food; it will then be found in the greatest abundance in the trachea and larger bronchi, whereas in those instances in which it has been in the tubes for some time before death the food will often have disappeared from the larger into the smaller tubes and air cells.

I have witnessed one case of fatal bronchitis in the horse, due to the entrance of vomited ingesta into the bronchi. Some days prior to its death fifteen minims of Fleming's tincture of aconite had been administered; this brought on attempts at vomition and great distress. The animal's respiration continued very highly accelerated after the effects of the aconite had passed off, and continued until the animal died. A *post-mortem* examination revealed the fact that vomition had occurred, and that the small quantity of food thus expelled had entered the larnyx and gained access to the bronchi.

ACUTE BRONCHITIS.·

Symptoms.—Bronchitis consists of congestion of the bronchial tissues, associated at first with dryness, narrowing, and rigidity, and subsequently moisture, dilatation, and relaxation of the tubes.

Owing to these changes, the vibrating sounds caused by the passage of air through the inflamed bronchi undergo variations, which indicate pretty clearly the dry or moist condition of the parts, or, as some term it, the dry or moist catarrh.

As the symptoms are developed, the cough becomes hoarse, ringing, loud, and paroxysmal; the respirations are in some instances greatly accelerated, indeed out of all proportion to the pulse. For example, the pulse may be seventy or eighty per minute, and the respirations as numerous, or even more so. This indicates bronchitis affecting the smaller tubes and alveolar walls—catarrhal pneumonia—collapse of a more or less extensive area of lung structure, or even occlusion of non-inflamed bronchi and air vesicles by the gravitation into them of the catarrhal fluid, as shown in the wood cut.

Bronchitis of the larger tubes is naturally less dangerous than the other two, and only proves fatal by inducing the two above-mentioned conditions, namely, collapse and occlusion of a more or less extensive breathing surface.

Amongst the foreign horses above alluded to, it was noticed, where the discharge of muco-purulent matter was most profuse, although some of the animals seemed to recover from the febrile disturbance and accelerated breathing of the acute stage, that they succumbed in from fourteen to thirty days afterwards from gangrene of the collapsed lungs, or putrefaction of the fluid incarcerated in the bronchi and air cells; both of these conditions being expressed by fœtor of the breath, exhaustive diarrhœas, metastatic inflammations of the articulations and feet, complete loss of appetite, rapid emaciation, fluttering pulse; at first great elevation of temperature—106° F. or more; partial sweats upon the body, gasping respiration, some abdominal pain, and other signs of general septicœmia.

In no case of pure bronchitis is the breathing painful, but short and quick, the thoracic as well as the abdominal muscles being brought into full play; this distinguishes it from the breathing characteristic of pleurisy, in which the ribs are more or less fixed and the respirations abdominal. In ordinary cases of bronchitis the animal is dull, listless, sometimes semi-comatose; hangs its head; is generally thirsty; ropy saliva fills the mouth, which is hot and moist. The visible mucous membranes are infected and present a varying degree of lividity, due to non-oxidation of the blood. The animal stands in a corner or moves listlessly about. If in a box, and the door be open, it stands with its head to the open air, from which it evidently obtains relief. The bowels are generally somewhat constipated, the feces covered with mucus, but they easily respond to purgatives, showing that the alimentary mucous membrane participates in the irritation. The urine is high-colored, scanty, and if examined will be found to contain urea, mucus, and coloring matter in excess, and the chlorides in diminished quantities.

As already stated, bronchitis of the larger tubes is not ordinarily a fatal disease, but when affecting the smaller bronchi and alveoli, particularly if associated with a profuse discharge of a yellowish-colored, more or less tenacious fluid, which occludes the smaller bronchi and air cells, it is the most fatal chest disease that the author is acquainted with. This tendency to gravitation of the catarrhal fluid is explained by the fact that the columnar and ciliated epithelium are shed in the earlier stage of the attack and take no part whatever in the after changes which ensue. It is never seen again till the signs of acute inflammation, such as distension of the vessels and œdema of the basement membrane have passed off. Subsequently it is gradually reproduced.—*Dr. Hamilton.*

The muco-purulent material thus incarcerated is driven or impacted by the ramrod-like action of the inspirated air into the periphery of the smaller tubes and vesicles, and there constitutes those masses which may undergo putrefaction in the horse, causing septicœmia, as already explained, and caseous masses, giving rise to tubercle in the ox.

The physical signs of bronchitis are as follows: Percussion returns a more or less resonant sound, but auscultation will enable the practitioner to detect the nature and extent of the bronchial inflammation. *Rhonchus*, confined to the upper and middle third of the chest, with true respiratory murmur over the lower part, will indicate inflammation of the larger and middle-sized bronchial tubes and a condition of comparatively little danger. *Sibilus*, heard at the lower parts, indicates a condition of much greater danger and that the disease involves the smaller tubes and air vesicles. Inspiration is generally shortened, expiration prolonged and more distinctly accompanied by the abnormal sounds. These sounds are succeeded at a later stage by moist bubbles, rattles, or rales—mucous rales. At first the discharge expelled by coughing is thick, tenacious, and gelatinous, or watery and scant. The lower animals do not, however, expectorate in the true sense of the word; some discharge issues from the nose, but the greater part of what is coughed up falls into the fauces and is swallowed. As the disease advances, however, a profuse discharge issues from the nostrils and the inflammation gradually subsides. The cough becomes less hoarse, more vigorous, and even more frequent than at first, but it gradually disappears; the discharge becomes again thinner, clearer, and eventually ceases.

In some instances all sounds disappear from a certain part of the lungs. This is due to occlusion of the tubes and vesicles by the catarrhal secretion, or to more or less collapse of the vesicular tissue, dependent on obstruction to the passage of air during inspiration by glutinous or inspissated mucus. This collapse is often confined to individual lobules, which are thus condensed, heavy, indurated, and of a dark color, and may ultimately become hepatized, atrophied, or even emphysematous.

PATHOLOGY AND MORBID ANATOMY.

Inflammation of the bronchial tubes, like that affecting other mucous membranes, is attended with changes in their epithelium, the secretion of the glands, and in the surrounding tissues.

It is rare to meet with a fatal case of bronchitis during its earlier stages, and but for the accidental slaughter in Liverpool of the American cattle already referred to, it would have been difficult to have given the details of the morbid anatomy.

The appearance of the lung in the earlier stage of bronchitis, with collapse, that is to say, when it is observed prior to the commencement of secondary changes or pneumonia, is as follows : There are patches over its surface that have fallen below the level of surrounding parts; sometimes these depressions measure an eighth of an inch in depth ; they are of a bluish purple color, and variable in size. The parts around them are of a light pink hue, and are either healthy or in a more or less emphysematous condition.

The depressions consist of certain lobules in a state of collapse arising from occlusion of their bronchial tubes by pus or other material. The collapsed portions are bluish-purple in color ; non-crepitant and depressed, resembling fetal lungs sinking slowly in water.

Collapse of the lung tissue, atelectasis, induces more or less congestion and subsequent inflammation ; consequently it is found that broncho-pneumonia often succeeds bronchitis, due to the absence of the expansion and contraction of the air vesicles which normally aid the pulmonary circulation, and to arrestment of the blood-flow, owing to imperfect aeration. This congestion is soon succeeded by effusion of serum, and the bluish-purple collapsed portions become darker in color and less resistant in consistence. They, however, retain some degree of elasticity, for, if not too rudely pulled out, they do not tear as in pleuro-pneumonia ; if cut into and exposed to the atmosphere for a few minutes the bluish-purple color becomes bright scarlet. It is important to bear in mind that the pneumonic process which supervenes in bronchitis is principally confined to those portions of the lungs in which collapse has taken place. Sometimes the collapse is isolated, invading but small portions of the lungs. This condition is not rarely witnessed in parasitic bronchial disease. These limited collapsed portions vary in size, are rather wedge-shaped, and have their apices towards the obstructed bronchus. The lung tissue surrounding them may be more or less congested, or it may be emphysematous, but no juice is exuded from them when cut into, as in acute pleuro-pneumonia.

Professor Gairdner was, I believe, the first to show that condensation of the vesicular substance occurs as a result of mucus or other obstruction in the air-tubes leading to the condensed portion. It is at first sight difficult to understand how incomplete obstructions of the bronchi—and these obtain much more frequently than absolutely complete occlusion—cause collapse. One would suppose that some quantity of air would gain access into the vesicles, but such is apparently not the case; and it seems that the air gradually finds its way out by the edges of the obstructing substance. The expiratory force, so long as there is air in the vesicles, constantly tends to dislodge the obstructing body by pushing it toward the wider (proximal) end of the tube, whilst the inspiratory drives it inwards toward the narrower tubes, which it effectually occludes. The entrance of air is thus more or less effectually opposed and its exit permitted, so that ultimately the vesicles beyond become completely emptied ; in fact, the plug acts as a valve, allowing the air to pass in one direction but opposing its passage in the other. Where the obstruction is complete from the commencement the air is absorbed.

It had been supposed by Laennec that the emphysema or, more correctly, over-distension with air of the parts surrounding the collapsed lobules was due to what he thought a fact, that the act of inspiration was more powerful than that of expiration ; so that though air could be drawn through the obstruction it could not be breathed out. In consequence, it accumulated in the ultimate pulmonary vesicles, became expanded by heat, and so acted mechanically as a dilator. Dr. Gairdner, however, pointed out that expiration is a much more powerful act than inspiration, and that there is never any difficulty in causing expulsion of air, provided always there be no obstruction in the tubes. Emphysema, then, does not occur in the vesicles connected with obstructed tubes, but in those which are adjacent. When the lungs are free from disease the column of air presses equally in all the tubes and vesicles ; but when one portion connected with any obstruction is collapsed, then the adjacent parts are over-expanded, so as to occupy the space previously filled by the former.

At a later stage the contents of the obstructed bronchi are pushed by the weight of the descending or inspired atmosphere into the most minute bronchi, alveoli, and air vesicles, always from the center towards the periphery, and appear as minute white points beneath the pleural surface. They are well shown in the figure.

On cutting into the lungs, it will be found that the large and small tubes, and sometimes the trachea, contain an amount of fluid. This condition, as well as the collapse, is limited in the majority of instances to the small or anterior lobes of the lungs, and rarely, except by extension, affects the large lobes, not only in ordinary but in mechanical bronchitis. This fact is of importance, as pleuro-pneumonia contagiosa, with which the disease under consideration has been confounded, generally commences in the larger lobes, either in their centers or towards their posterior edges.

The fluid contained in the tubes is thick and has a yellow color ; in the trachea it is more or less frothy ; and is abundant in the smaller bronchi, as shown in the figure.

If the lungs in this condition be squeezed, little pellets of yellow matter are pressed out. Sometimes these pellets are too small to be seen by the naked eye, and require the aid of a magnifying glass. If the bronchitis be associated with catarrhal pneumonia, elevated patches will be apparent on the cut surface, having a grayish-red color. They are soft to the touch, and if squeezed the same muco-purulent matter exudes from them, or from a small bronchus which may happen to communicate with the particular group of vesicles implicated.

Dr. Hamilton, in his series of papers on bronchitis, published in the *Practitioner* for 1879, states it is a matter of difficulty in man to get at the first change which ensues in the bronchi in acute catarrh. He has, however, been able to verify his observations by an examination along with myself of the lungs of American cattle slaughtered in the earlier stages of bronchitis; in fact before any external signs of disease were manifested. He says, "On careful comparison, however, of many cases, we feel assured that the first deviation visible is a *relaxation and distension of the abundant plexus of blood-vessels ramifying in the inner fibrous coat*, immediately beneath the basement membrane—that is to say, of the branches of the bronchial artery. They become engorged with blood, so that on transverse section they appear like little cavities distended with blood corpuscles. In a few hours afterward the basement membrane* becomes much more apparent than it usually is, and at the same time more clear and homogeneous, while the surface is thrown into many folds. These changes in the basement membrane are apparently due to its becoming œdematous, serous fluid being infiltrated into it from the underlying plexus of distended vessels; and we shall see that, as the acute irritation continues, this œdematous state of the basement membrane becomes more and more a well-marked feature. The next change, so far as we, have been able to calculate, occurs in from twenty to thirty hours after the primary distension of the vessels, and consists in the loosening and desquamation of the columnar epithelium at the foci of greatest congestion.

"The columnar epithelium is thus shed at a very early stage of the attack, and takes no part whatever in the after changes which ensue. It is never seen again until the other signs of acute inflammation, such as the distension of the vessels and œdema of the basment membrane have passed off. Subsequently we shall see that it is gradually reproduced. The cause of this desquamation of the columnar epithelium seems to be the œdema of the basment membrane loosening its underlying attachments, very much in the same way as the vesicles which form in an acute inflammatory affection of the skin loosen the attachments of the superficial layer of epidermis. The removal of this protective covering from the mucous membrane naturally leaves the latter in an exposed condition, and no doubt the feeling of rawness experienced in acute catarrh of the bronchi is due to the cold air acting upon an over-stimulated and exposed mucous membrane. And, further, it can easily be understood that, where this desquamation takes place to an inordinately great extent, the loss of the ciliary action of the columnar cells will seriously interfere with expectoration, and tend to cause the catarrhal products to gravitate downward towards the smaller bronchi and air vesicles. This description essentially coincides with what Socoloff found experimentally in animals (Virchow's *Archiv.*, vol. 68, p. 611), in which he induced an artificial bronchitis by the injection of irritants, such as potassic bichromate, into the air passages. He states that one of the first changes which ensued was the desquamation of the columnar cells, and that they took no part in the catarrhal inflammatory process." This early shedding of the columnar cells, and their non-reproduction until after the subsidence of the inflammatory process, is a fact of real importance, as it goes a long way to explain the occurrence of those caseous tumors which give rise to tubercle, and are so often confounded with that growth.

The pneumonic process, which may supervene either by extension of the inflammatory process from the tubes to the alveoli or the irritation of inhaled inflammatory products subsequent to collapse, is, in the earlier stage, commonly limited to scattered groups of air-vesicles; hence the term "lobular" which is applied to it. It causes the portions affected to appear as scattered, ill-defined nodules of consolidation, irregular in size, and passing insensibly into the surrounding tissue, which is variously altered by collapse, emphysema, and congestion. These nodules are of a reddish-gray color, faintly granular or smooth, slightly elevated, and soft in consistence. As they increase in size they may become confluent; and in a more advanced stage they become paler, drier, firmer, and, to some extent, resemble ordinary gray hepatization. Microscopically examined, they are seen to consist of cellular elements accumulated in the alveoli.

The disease may, as already remarked, terminate fatally by the absorption of the putrescent catarrhal products, by gangrene of the collapsed lungs, or by sudden effusion of fluid into the bronchi, constituting what is termed "suffocative catarrh." If a fatal termination does not ensue the contents of the alveoli undergo degeneration and are gradually removed by discharge, or by absorption, or by coalescence form caseous masses, which may become encapsuled, undergo the calcareous change, and thus become innocuous; or may induce a diathesis, leading to the actual development of

---

*The basement membrane is not so apparent in the lower animals as in man.

Plate II.

Drawings showing comparative appearances of PLEURO PNEUMONIA (CONTAGIOSA AND BRONCHITIS.

A. PLEURO PNEUMONIA
After Prof. W. Williams.

1.
External aspect, with
exudation on pleural surface.

II. Internal aspect of same lung, showing marbled condition.

Plate III.

B. BRONCHITIS. (Earliest Stage).

After Prof. W. Williams.

External aspect
some of the
lobules in a state of
collapse from occlusion of bronchi.

II. Internal aspect of same, bronchi filled with catarrhal products.

Plate IV.

Contagious Pleuro-Pneumonia of Cattle.

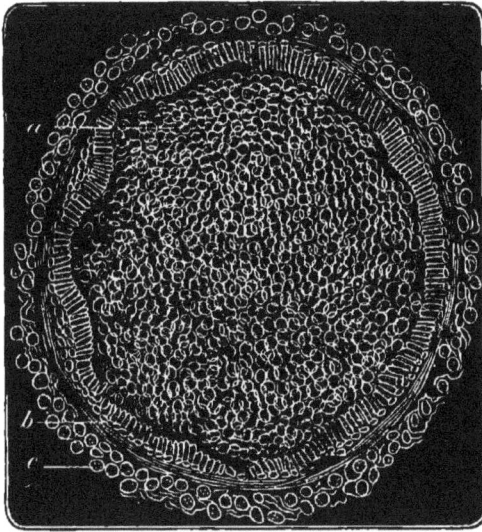

Fig.1.- Small bronchus in acute bronchitis, occluded by a plug of catarrhal secretion.-350 diam. a, Catarrhal plug; b. Epithelium lining bronchus; c. Surrounding adventitious coat infiltrated with cells.-(From American ox condemned at Liverpool for pleuro-pneumonia.)

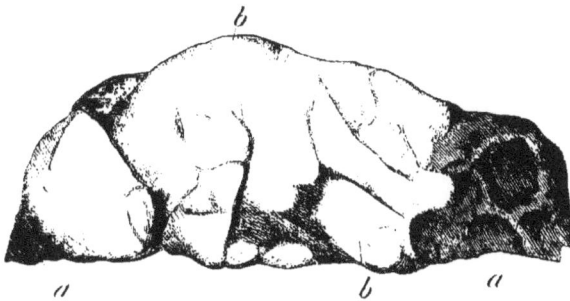

Fig.2.- Portion of lung from American ox slaughtered at Liverpool, and showing bronchitis in the very earliest stages (a a, collapsed lobules) from obstruction of tubes. The elevations (b b, non collapsed lobules) are slightly emphysematous.

A. Hoen & Co. Lithocaustic, Baltimore

Plate V.

Contagious Pleuro-Pneumonia of Cattle.

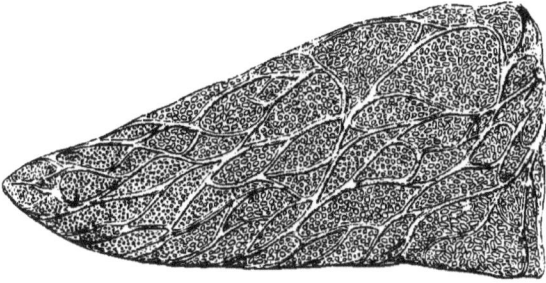

Fig. 3.—*Pleural aspect of pulmonary lobe from American ox
slaughtered at Liverpool; alveoli filled with muco-purulent
matter; pleural surface intact. The microscopic examination revealed broncho-pneumonia in some of the alveoli
(see fig 6) whilst others showed no traces of inflammation
(see fig.1), but were merely filled with the inhaled bronchial
secretions.*

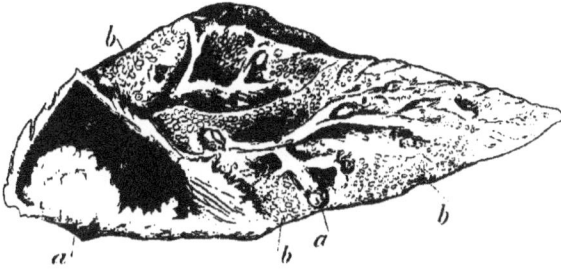

Fig. 4.—*Section of portion of lung; the external aspect is shown
in fig.3. The larger (a) and smaller bronchi and air vesicles
(b) filled with purulent matter.*

Plate VI.

Contagious Pleuro-Pneumonia of Cattle.

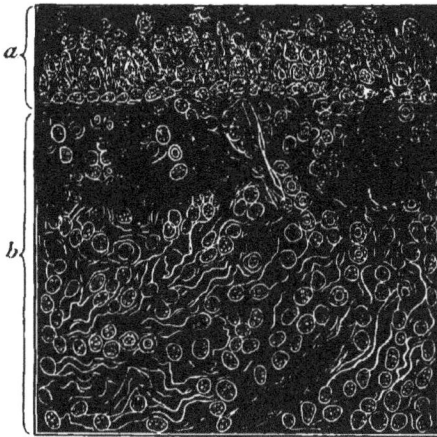

Fig. 5.—Bronchus (medium sized) in acute bronchitis—(American ox slaughtered at Liverpool.)
(a) Deep layer of epithelium, germinating and throwing off catarrhal cells.
(b) Inner fibrous coat, infiltrated with inflammatory cells. (480 diam.) The columnar epithelium shed.

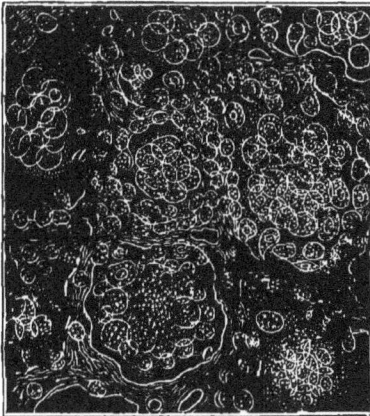

Fig. 6.—. Acute catarrhal pneumonia (. American ox).—Section through several air vesicles. Shows the alveolar cavities filled with large granular catarrhal cells (c). (b) Catarrhal cells sprouting from the alveolar wall. (a) Coagulated mucus in which the catarrhal cells lie.—(480 diam.)

A. Hoen & Co. Lithocaustic Baltimore.

tubercle in the ox and to symptoms simulating phthisis pulmonalis in the horse; that is to say, an accumulation of catarrhal products, epithelial and other cells within the pulmonary alveoli, cellular infiltration and thickening of the walls of the alveoli and bronchi, increase in the interlobular connective tissue, with, in some instances, the occurrence of fibrinous masses intermixed with leucocytes in the alveoli, as demonstrated by Zenker, of Dresden, but without—except very rarely, indeed, in the horse—the occurrence of tubercular tumors (grapes) in the serous membranes and parenchyma of organs.

In all cases of bronchitis the bronchial glands undergo some change. In the earlier stages they are increased in size, contain the products of the bronchitis conveyed by the lymph tract, become more or less friable in consistence, and in more advanced bronchial inflammation distended with catarrhal elements, both glands and contents undergoing the caseous metamorphosis, the products of which may either liquefy or become infiltrated with calcareous matter.

THE CONTAGIOUS DISEASES (ANIMALS) ACT, 32 AND 33 VICT., AND ORDERS FOR GREAT BRITAIN.

CHAPTER 70.—An act to consolidate, amend, and make perpetual the acts for preventing the introduction or spreading of contagious diseases among cattle and other animals in Great Britain. [9th August, 1869.]

Whereas, it is expedient to confer on Her Majesty's most honorable privy council power to take such measures as may appear from time to time necessary to prevent the introduction into Great Britain of contagious or infectious diseases among cattle, sheep, and other animals, by prohibiting or regulating the importation of foreign animals; and it is further expedient to provide against the spreading of such diseases in Great Britain, and to consolidate and amend and make perpetual the acts relating thereto, and to make such other provisions as are contained in this act:

Be it therefore enacted by the Queen's Most Excellent Majesty, by and with the advice and consent of the lords spiritual and temporal and commons, in this present Parliament assembled, and by the authority of the same, as follows:

PART I.—PRELIMINARY.]

1. This act may be cited as the contagious diseases (animals) act, 1869.
2. This act shall not extend to Ireland.
3. This act is divided into parts, as follows:
Part   I.—Preliminary.
Part   II.—Local authorities.
Part   III.—Foreign animals.
Part   IV.—Discovery and prevention of diseases.
Part   V.—Slaughter in cattle-plague: compensation.
Part   VI.—Orders of council and of local authorities.
Part   VII.—Lands.
Part VIII.—Expenses of local authorities.
Part   IX.—Offenses and legal proceedings.
Part   X.—Scotland.
4. The acts described in the first schedule to this act are hereby repealed; but this repeal shall not extend to Ireland, or affect the past operation of any of those acts, or affect any order of Her Majesty in council made, or any order or regulation of the privy council or of a local authority made, or any license granted, or any committee or subcommittee constituted, or any appointment made, or any right, title, obligation or liability accrued, or any rate or mortgage made, or the validity or invalidity of anything done or suffered under any of those acts before the passing of this act; nor shall this repeal interfere with the institution or prosecution of any proceeding in respect of any offense committed against, or any penalty or forfeiture incurred under, any of the acts repealed by this act, or any order or regulation made thereunder, or take away or abridge any protection conferred or secured by any of those acts in relation to anything done thereunder before the passing of this act; and notwithstanding the repeal by this act of any of those acts, every local authority constituted thereby or thereunder shall (subject to any provision of this act altering the local authority or the constitution thereof in any case) continue as if this act had not been passed; and every such order, regulation, license, subcommittee, and appointment, as aforesaid, shall continue and be as if this act had not been passed; but so that the same may be revoked, altered, or otherwise dealt with under this act, as if the same had been made, granted, or constituted under this act.

5. In this act the term "the privy council" means the lords and others of Her Majesty's most honorable privy council.

All or any powers by this act conferred on the privy council may be exercised by those lords and others, or any two or more of them.

Powers by this act conferred on the privy council may, as regards the making of orders affecting only specified ports, towns, or places, or parts thereof, and as regards the issuing and revocation of licenses under any order of council, be exercised by the lord president of the council, or one of Her Majesty's principal secretaries of state.

6. In this act—

The term "cattle" means bulls, cows, oxen, heifers, and calves.

The term "animal" means, except where it is otherwise expressed, cattle, sheep, goats, and swine.

The term "foreign," as applied to cattle or animals, means brought from any place out of the United Kingdom.

The term "cattle plague" means the rinderpest, or disease commonly called the cattle plague.

The term "contagious or infectious disease" includes cattle plague, pleuro-pneumonia, foot-and-mouth disease, sheep-pox, sheep-scab, and glanders,* and any disease which the privy council from time to time by order declares to be a contagious or infectious disease for the purposes of this act.

The term "railway company" includes a company or person working a railway, under lease or otherwise.

The term "person" includes a body corporate or unincorporate.

7. In this act—

The term "borough" means a place which is for the time being subject to the act of the session of the fifth and sixth years of the reign of King William the Fourth (chapter 76), "to provide for the regulation of municipal corporations in England and Wales," or which is a town or place having under any general or local act of Parliament or otherwise a separate police establishment.

The term "county" does not include a county of a city or county of a town, but includes any riding division or parts of a county, having a separate commission of the peace.

The term "metropolis" includes all parishes and places in which the metropolitan board of works have or had power to levy a main drainage rate.

For the purposes of this act, the liberty of St. Albans, the liberty of the Isle of Ely, and the soke of Peterborough shall, respectively, be deemed separate counties; but all other liberties and franchises of counties shall be considered as forming part of the county by which they are surrounded; or if partly surrounded by two or more counties, then as forming part of that county with which they have the longest common boundary.

Every place that is not a borough, a county, or part of the metropolis, as respectively defined in this act, or is not separately mentioned in the second schedule to this act, shall be deemed to form part of a county, as defined in this act, to the county rate whereof it is assessed; or if it is not so assessed, then of the county within which it is situate.

8. The schedules to this act shall be construed and have effect as part of this act.

PART II.—LOCAL AUTHORITIES.

9. For the purposes of this act, the respective districts, authorities, rates or funds, and officers described in the second schedule to this act shall be the district, the local authority, the local rate, and the clerk of the local authority.

Notwithstanding anything in this act, or the second schedule thereto, within the city of London and the liberties thereof the mayor, aldermen, and commons of the city of

---

* By an order of council (365) dated 30th June, 1873, it was enacted that, after the 2d day of July 1873—

"Farcy is hereby declared to be a contagious disease for the purposes of the act of 1869, and all the provisions relating to contagious or infectious diseases contained in any order of council for the time being in force thereunder shall also apply to farcy.

"Where a local authority is authorized by the privy council to make regulations for the purpose of preventing the spread of glanders and farcy, or either of them, the local authority may make regulations for the following purposes, or any of them:

"For prohibiting or regulating the movement out of any field, stable, shed, or other premises in which glanders or farcy has been found to exist, of any horse that is, or has been, affected with glanders or farcy, or that has been in the same field, stable, shed, or other premises with or in contact with any horse affected with glanders or farcy."

Another order in council, dated 7th of August, 1874, states that this of 1873. "Shall have effect as if in article 2 thereof the words glanders and farcy were substituted for the words contagious and infectious."

The committee on this act, in August, 1873, recommended "that the slaughter of horses affected with glanders should be compulsory, but that payment should be made to the owner for the value of the carcasses."

London shall be the local authority, and the town clerk shall be the clerk of the local authority, and the consolidated rate shall be the local rate; but the city of London and the liberties thereof shall nevertheless be deemed part of the metropolis for the purposes of the local rate described in the second schedule to this act in relation to the metropolis.

11. With respect to committees of a local authority, the following provisions shall have effect:

(1.) A local authority shall form a committee or committees, and may delegate to any such committee all or any powers conferred on the local authority by this act, except the power to make a rate.

(2.) A local authority may from time to time revoke or alter any power given by them to a committee.

(3.) A local authority may appoint and designate any such committee as their executive committee for the purposes of this act.

(4.) Such an executive committee shall have all the powers of the local authority under this act, except the power to make a rate, and may appoint a subcommittee or subcommittees, and delegate to them all or any powers of the executive committee, with or without conditions or restrictions, and from time to time revoke or alter any such delegation, and fix the quorum, and add to or diminish the number of the members, or otherwise alter the constitution of a subcommittee, and lay down rules for the guidance of a subcommittee, who shall act accordingly.

(5.) Proceedings of a committee or subcommittee shall not be invalidated by any vacancy in the committee or subcommittee, or, in case of a committee appointed by general or quarter sessions of a county, by the termination of the sessions at which they were appointed.

(6.) In case of the formation of two or more committees, they shall act according to rules laid down for their guidance by the local authority.

(7.) The regulations contained in the third schedule to this act shall have effect with respect to the committees and subcommittees.

Inspectors and officers.

12. Every local authority shall from time to time appoint so many inspectors and other officers as appear to the local authority necessary for the execution of this act, and shall assign them such duties and award them such salaries or allowances as the local authority think fit, and may at any time revoke any appointment so made, but so that every local authority shall at all times keep appointed at least one inspector.

13. The privy council, if satisfied on inquiry that an inspector appointed by a local authority is incompetent, or has been guilty of misconduct or neglect in the discharge of his duty, may, if they think fit, direct his removal, and thereupon he shall cease to be an inspector for the purposes of this act.

14. Every local authority, and every inspector appointed by a local authority, shall make such reports to the privy council as the privy council may from time to time require.

PART III.—FOREIGN ANIMALS.

15. The privy council may from time to time by order define the limits of ports for the purpose of this part of this act.

16. The privy council may from time to time by order, in relation to foreign animals, or to any specified kind of foreign animals, or to foreign animals, or any specified kind thereof, brought from any specified country or place, prohibit the landing thereof either generally, or in any specified port, or in any defined part thereof, or elsewhere than in some specified port or ports, or than in some defined part or parts thereof.

This section shall extend to horses and other animals not within the definition of animals in this act.

17. The privy council may from time to time by order apply to the landing, either generally or with specified exceptions, or in some specified port, or in some defined part thereof, of foreign animals, or of any specified kind of foreign animals, or of foreign animals, or any specified kind thereof, brought from any specified country or place, and to the movement and disposal thereof when landed, the regulations contained in the fourth schedule to this act, or any of them.

18. The privy council may from time to time by order, in relation to foreign animals or to any specified kind of foreign animals, or to foreign animals or any specified kind thereof, brought from any specified country or place, add to or vary the regulations contained in the fourth schedule to this act.

19. Where the regulations contained in the fourth schedule to this act, or any of them (with or without addition or variations,) are in operation in respect of a port or a defined part thereof, then all animals for the time being within that port or defined part shall, subject to any order of the privy council to the contrary, be deemed foreign animals, and the same regulations shall apply thereto accordingly.

20. The privy council may from time to time by order make such regulations as they think expedient for imposing conditions on the landing of or for subjecting to inspection or to quarantine foreign animals, or any specified kind of foreign animals, or foreign animals, or any specified kind thereof brought from any specified country or place.

This section shall extend to horses and other animals not within the definition of animals in this act.

21. If any person lands or attempts to land any foreign animal (including any horse or other animal not within the definition of animals in this act) in contravention of any order of the privy council, the animals shall be forfeited in like manner as goods the importation whereof is hereby prohibited by the acts relating to the customs are liable to be forfeited, and the person so offending shall be liable to such penalties as are imposed on persons importing or attempting to import goods the importation whereof is prohibited by the acts relating to the customs, without prejudice to any proceeding against him under this act or any such order, but so that no person be punished twice for the same offense.

Article 9 of order in council (341), dated December 20, 1871, specifies that "animals landed from a vessel shall, on a certificate of an inspector appointed by the privy council in that behalf, certifying to the effect that the foregoing regulations, or some or one of them, have not or has not been observed in the vessel, be detained at the landing-place, or in lairs adjacent thereto, until the privy council otherwise direct."

22. There shall be published in the London Gazette, once in every month, under the direction of the privy council, a return of the number of foreign animals brought by sea to any port in Great Britain, which on inspection on landing within the then last preceding month have been found to be affected with any contagious or infectious disease, specifying the disease and the ports from which and to which such animals are brought, and the mode in which such animals have been disposed of.

23. A local authority may provide, erect, and fit up wharves, lairs, sheds, markets, houses, and places for the landing, reception, sale, and slaughter of foreign animals.

24. There shall be incorporated with this part of this act the markets and fairs clauses act, 1847; and, for the purposes of the application and construction of that act in conjunction with this part of this act, any place provided by a local authority under this part of this act for the landing, reception, sale, or slaughter of foreign animals shall be deemed a market, and this part of this act shall be deemed the special act, and the prescribed limits shall be deemed to be the limits of the lands acquired for the purposes of this part of this act; and by-laws shall be approved by the privy council, which approval shall be sufficient without any other approval or any allowance thereof (notice of application for such approval being nevertheless given, and proposed by-laws being published before application for approval, in like manner as under that act, notice of application for allowance and publication before that application are required to be made).

25. A local authority may charge for the use of any wharf, lair, shed, market, house, or place provided by them under this part of this act, such sums as they from time to time by by-laws appoint.

26. A local authority, on exercising for the purposes of this part of this act the borrowing powers vested in them under this act, may, if they think fit, give as security for repayment of money borrowed with interest (either together with the local rate, if any, or separately therefrom) the charges which they are authorized to make under this part of this act, and any estates, revenues, or funds belonging to them and not otherwise appropriated by law.

27. All money received by a local authority from charges made by them under this part of this act shall be carried to a separate account, and shall be applied in payment of interest on money borrowed by them for the purposes of this part of this act, and in repayment of the principal thereof, and subject thereto towards discharge of expenses incurred by them in the execution of this act.

1. *By an order in council (342) of December 20, 1871, additional regulations are laid down with regard to foreign cattle, and which were to take effect from the 31st of that month.*

2. This order may be cited as the foreign animals order of 1871.

3. This order extends to Great Britain only.

4. In this order—

The act of 1869 means the contagious diseases (animals) act, 1869.

A defined part of a port means a part of a port defined by a special order of the privy council in pursuance of regulations 2 of the fourth schedule to the act of 1869.

Landing-place for slaughter means a landing-place within a defined part of a port.

Master includes any person having the charge or command of a vessel.

Other terms, except when otherwise expressed, have the same meaning as in the act of 1869.

5. Foreign animals shall not be landed at any place except the ports comprised in the first schedule in this order.

6. Foreign animals landed at any port shall be landed in such manner, within such times, and subject to such supervision and control as the commissioners of Her Majesty's customs from time to time direct, and when landed shall be placed under the charge of a veterinary inspector appointed in that behalf by the privy council, and shall be dealt with in accordance with the instructions from time to time given by the privy council.

7. Foreign animals shall, except as in this order provided, be detained for at least twelve hours after landing in some lair or other proper place adjacent to the landing-place, and shall be inspected by the veterinary inspector of the privy council.

8. Where one part of a cargo of foreign animals is landed at one place and another part is landed at another place, or where parts of a cargo of foreign animals are landed at different times at the same place, twelve hours' detention shall commence from the time of the landing of the last animal of the cargo; and if any contagious or infectious disease is detected in any animal of the cargo, every animal in each separate part of the cargo shall be dealt with as if the disease had been detected in an animal in each separate part.

9. Where any foreign animal forming part of one cargo has not been kept separate from any foreign animal forming part of another cargo, all the foreign animals forming such cargoes shall be treated as forming one cargo.

10. A veterinary inspector of the privy council may detain, for any period that he thinks necessary or proper, any foreign animals (including horses and other animals not within the definition of animals in the act of 1869) which he has reason to suspect are affected with any contagious or infectious disease, or may introduce any such disease.

11. If any foreign sheep or swine are found to be affected with any contagious or infectious disease (except cattle plague) such sheep or swine shall be kept separate from those of the same cargo not found to be so affected ; and the slaughter of those not found to be so affected may, with the permission of the veterinary inspector of the privy council, be begun at any time before the expiration of the twelve hours' detention, and be continued without intermission.

12. No animal, carcass, hide, meat, or offal, and no hay, straw, litter, or other things commonly used for food of animals, or otherwise for or about animals, and no dung, shall be removed from their lair or other place adjacent to the landing place where foreign animals are detained, except with the permission of the veterinary inspector of the privy council, and, if the inspector is of opinion that any such animal or thing as aforesaid may introduce any contagious or infectious disease, the same shall be slaughtered, destroyed, or otherwise dealt with in accordance with the instructions from time to time given by the privy council.

13. Subject to any provision in this or any other order to the contrary, all the regulations in the fourth schedule to the act of 1869 shall apply to cattle brought from any port or any of the countries comprised in the second schedule to this order; and, subject as aforesaid, all such cattle shall be slaughtered within ten days after the landing thereof, exclusive of the day of landing.

14. The landing of foreign cattle elsewhere than at a landing place for slaughter shall be subject to the following conditions :

First. That the vessel in which they are imported has not, within three months before taking them on board, had on board any cattle exported from any port of any of the countries comprised in the second schedule to this order.

Secondly. That the vessel has not, since taking on board the cattle imported, entered any port of any of those countries.

Thirdly. That the cattle imported have not, while on board the vessel, been in contact with any cattle exported from any port of any of those countries.

And foreign cattle shall not be landed elsewhere than at a landing place for slaughter, unless and until—

(1.) The owner or charterer of the vessel in which they are imported, or his agent in Great Britain, has entered into a bond to Her Majesty the Queen, in a sum not exceeding one thousand pounds, with or without a surety or sureties, to the satisfaction of the commissioners of Her Majesty's customs, conditioned for the observance of the foregoing conditions in relation to cattle to be landed under this order from the vessel ; and

(2.) The master of the vessel has on each occasion of importation of cattle therein satisfied the commissioners of Her Majesty's customs or their proper officer, by declaration made and signed or otherwise, that none of the cattle then imported therein have been exported from any port of any of the countries comprised in the second schedule to this order, and that the foregoing conditions have been observed in relation to all the cattle then imported therein.

15. Foreign animals landed from a vessel elsewhere than at a landing place for slaughter shall not be moved therefrom or be allowed to come in contact with any other animals until they have been examined by the veterinary inspector appointed in

S. Ex. 5——4

that behalf by the privy council, and according to the result of such inspection the following consequences shall ensue :

(1.) If the inspector certifies that all the animals landed from the vessel are free from contagious or infectious disease, they shall thereupon cease to be deemed foreign animals.

(2.) If the inspector certifies, with respect to any one or more of the animals landed from the vessel, that it or they is or are affected with any contagious or infectious disease, all the animals then imported in the vessel shall be slaughtered or otherwise dealt with in accordance with the instructions from time to time given by the privy council.

16. The regulations of the fourth schedule to the act of 1869 shall not apply to any milch cow brought from a port of any of the countries comprised in the second schedule to this order, provided the commissioners of Her Majesty's customs are, on each occasion of the same being so brought, satisfied that the same had been taken from Great Britain to that port, and has not been landed at that port or at any other port of any of those countries; and in relation to the landing, on any occasion, of any such milch cow in Great Britain elsewhere than at a landing place for slaughter, the condition that the vessel has not, since taking on board the cattle imported, entered any port of any of those countries, shall not operate provided the commissioners of Her Majesty's customs are on each occasion satisfied as aforesaid ; and the twelve hours' detention may be enforced on board the vessel.

17. In the case of a foreign animal which is brought in a vessel from any country other than those comprised in the second schedule to this order, but which was not taken on board for importation into Great Britain, the twelve hours' detention may be enforced on board the vessel.

18. If a vessel arriving at a port has on board the carcass of a foreign animal (including a horse) which was taken on board for the purpose of importation, but has died on the voyage, the master of the vessel shall, immediately on arrival, report the fact to the principal officer of Her Majesty's customs at the port.

No such carcass shall be landed or discharged from the vessel without the permission in writing of the principal officer.

19. Where it appears to the principal officer of Her Majesty's customs at a port, with respect to any foreign animal (including a horse or other animal not within the definition of animals in the act of 1869), or any hay, straw, fodder, or other article, brought by sea to the port, that contagion or infection may be thereby conveyed to animals, he may seize and detain the same, and he shall forthwith report the facts to the commissioners of Her Majesty's customs, who may give such directions as they think fit, either for the slaughter or destruction or the further detention thereof, or for the restoration thereof to the owner on such conditions, if any (including payment by the owner of expenses incurred by them in respect of detention thereof), as they think fit.

20. Foreign cattle, sheep, goats, and swine, in a defined part of a port (except sheep, goats, and swine in a defined part of the port of London) shall be marked as follows :

Cattle.—By clipping a broad arrow, about five inches long, on the left quarter (in addition to clipping the hair off the end of the tail, as prescribed by regulation 4 of the fourth schedule to the act of 1869).

Sheep and goats.—By clipping a broad arrow, about four inches long, on the forehead.

Swine.—By printing a broad arrow, about three inches long, on the left side with the following composition, namely : Rosin, five parts; oil of turpentine, two parts; and red ocher, one part; melted and use warm.

21. Where any regulation relating to foreign animals is in operation, the local authority and all constables and police officers shall assist the veterinary inspector of the privy council to carry the same into effect and to enforce the same, and shall do or cause to be done all things from time to time necessary for the effectual execution of the same.

22. A person for the time being appointed by the privy council an inspector, for the purposes of the act of 1869, shall have at every port all such powers, authorities, and privileges as a veterinary inspector specially appointed by the privy council for the inspection of foreign animals has at any specified port.

23. In paragraph 5 of the fourth schedule to the act of 1869, the words privy council shall be deemed to be substituted for the words commissioners of customs.

24. For the explanation and amendment of certain orders of council having a local operation only, the following provisions shall have effect :

(1.) Any defined part of a port for cattle shall be deemed a defined part of the same port for animals.

(2.) In the order of the 1st day of October, 1870, defining parts of the port of Southampton, the words, "the veterinary inspector appointed in that behalf by the privy council" shall be deemed to be substituted for the words "an officer of customs."

In an order in council, of August 7, 1874, cited as the "animals (amendment) order of 1874," the words of which were to have the same meaning as in the act of 1869, it

CONTAGIOUS DISEASES OF CATTLE. 51

is stated that (3) the foreign animals order of 1871 "has and shall have effect subject and by way of supplement to the animals order of 1871; and nothing in the foreign animals order of 1871 interferes or shall interfere with the execution or discharge by the local authority, or the inspector or other officer of the local authority, of any power or duty conferred or imposed on them or him by the act of 1869, or by any order of council." It also states that (4) "Regulation 7 of the fourth schedule to the act of 1869, shall apply in every case where a vessel comes into port having on board foreign animals maimed or injured on the voyage ; but notwithstanding anything in section nineteen of the act of 1869, any animals being at any time within such port shall not be deemed foreign animals by reason only of anything in this order."

An order in council (351) further regulates the importation of cattle from Russia. It is dated July 19, 1872, and specifies—

1. This order shall take effect from and immediately after the nineteenth day of July, one thousand eight hundred and seventy-two ; and words in this order have the same meaning as in the act of 1869.

2. Cattle brought from any place in the dominions of the Emperor of Russia shall not be landed at any port or place in Great Britain.

3. The following articles brought from any place in the dominions of the Emperor of Russia shall not be landed at any port or place in Great Britain: Manure or hay.

4. The following articles brought from any place in the dominions of the Emperor of Russia shall not be landed at any port or place in Great Britain, except at the ports at which foreign animals may be landed, and shall not be removed from the place where landed without a certificate of an inspector of the privy council, certifying that such articles are not likely to introduce any contagious or infectious disease : Meat, hides, fat, hoofs, or horns.

5. Subject to the provisions contained in the orders of council relating to the ports of Granton and Leith, dated the tenth day of August, one thousand eight hundred and sixty-nine, and in the order of council relating to the port of Southampton, dated the first day of October, one thousand eight hundred and seventy, all the regulations in the fourth schedule to the act of 1869 shall apply to sheep and goats brought to Great Britain from any place in the dominions of the Emperor of Russia, and landed in Great Britain, and all such sheep and goats shall be slaughtered within ten days after the landing thereof, exclusive of the day of landing ; provided, nevertheless, that cattle, sheep or goats being or having been on board any vessel at the same time with any cattle brought from any place in the dominions of the Emperor of Russia shall not be landed at any port or place in Great Britain.

6. Notwithstanding any order of council to the contrary, no sheep or goats brought from any place in the dominions of the Emperor of Russia, and landed within the port of London shall be moved alive out of any part of the port defined as a part within which foreign cattle may be landed for slaughter.

An order of council (364) dated July 11, 1873, regulates the tariff in cattle with Schleswig-Holstein. It says:

1. This order shall take effect from and immediately after the twenty-third day of June, one thousand eight hundred and seventy-three, and shall cease to have effect from and immediately after the thirtieth day of November, one thousand eight hundred and seventy-three.

2. This order may be cited as the Schleswig-Holstein order of 1873.

3. This order extends to Great Britain only.

4. In this order—

The act of 1869 means the contagious diseases (animals) act, 1869.

A defined part of a port means a part of a port defined by a special order of the privy council in pursuance of regulation 2 of the fourth schedule to the act of 1869.

Landing place for slaughter means a landing place within a defined part of a port.

Master includes any person having the charge or command of a vessel.

Other terms have the same meaning as in the act of 1869.

5. Notwithstanding anything in the foreign animals order of 1871, the regulations in the fourth schedule to the act of 1869 shall not apply to cattle brought from a port in either of the parts of the Empire of Germany respectively known as Schleswig and Holstein.

6. Cattle brought from a port of Schleswig or of Holstein shall not be landed elsewhere than at a landing-place for slaughter, unless and until the owner, agent, or charterer of the vessel in which they are brought has received the special permission of the privy council to employ the vessel in the trade of importation of cattle from ports of Schleswig and of Holstein, or of either of them, under this order.

7. The landing of cattle brought from a port of Schleswig or of Holstein, elsewhere than at a landing-place for slaughter, shall be subject to the following conditions :

First. That the vessel in which they are imported has not, within three months before taking them on board, had on board any cattle exported from any port in any part of the Empire of Germany, other than Schleswig or Holstein, or from any port of any of the following countries, namely : The dominions of the Emperor of Russia, tho Austrian-Hungarian Empire, the dominions of the Sultan, the dominions of the King of Italy, the dominions of the King of tho Hellenes, Belgium, France.

Secondly. That the vessel has not, since taking on board tho cattle imported, entered any such port as aforesaid.

Thirdly. That the cattle imported have not, while on board the vessel, been in contact with any cattle exported from any such port as aforesaid.

Fourthly. That the cattle imported are accompanied by a declaration and certificates, such as are indited in the forms set forth in the schedule to this order, or to the like effect.

8. Further, cattle brought from a port of Schleswig or of Holstein shall not be landed elsewhere than at a landing-place for slaughter, unless and until—

(1.) The owner or charterer of the vessel in which they are imported, or his agent in Great Britain, has entered into a bond to Her Majesty the Queen, in a sum not exceeding one thousand pounds with or without a surety or sureties to the satisfaction of the commissioners of Her Majesty's customs, conditioned for the observance of the foregoing conditions in relation to cattle to be landed under this order from the vessels; and

(2.) The master of the vessel has on each occasion of importation of cattle therein satisfied the commissioners of Her Majesty's customs, or their proper officer, by declaration made and signed or otherwise, that none of the cattle then imported therein have been exported from any port in any part of the Empire of Germany, other than Schleswig or Holstein, or from any port of any of the other countries named in article 7, of this order, and that the foregoing conditions have been observed in relation to all the cattle then imported therein.

9. If the veterinary inspector of the privy council is of opinion, on the examination of any cattle imported under this order, that the declaration accompanying the cattle is untrue in any particular as regards any one of the cattle in the vessel, then all the animals in the vessel shall be detained and dealt with in accordance with instructions from time to time given by the privy council.

10. If the declaration accompanying any cattle imported under this order is untrue in any particular as regards any one of the cattle to which it relates, the master of the vessel shall be guilty of an offense against this order, unless he shows to the satisfaction of the justices before whom he is charged that he did not know of the same being so untrue, and that ho could not with reasonable diligence have obtained such knowledge.

11. Subjects to the provisions of this order all the provisions of the foreign animals order of 1871 shall continue to apply to cattle brought from a port of Schleswig or of Holstein.

SCHEDULE.

Declaration and certificates.

DECLARATION.

I, *A. B.*, of ——, being the agent for the owners [or charterers] of the vessel ——, of ——, hereby solemnly and sincerely declare to the best of my knowledge and belief, that each of the cattle described below, now about to be put on board the said vessel, has been bred and fed exclusively in Denmark, Schleswig, and Holstein, or some or one of them, and has never been in contact with cattle not so exclusively bred and fed.

Dated this —— day of ——.
(To be signed.)   A. B.
Description of cattle above referred to :
                                                                                      *Number.

Bulls .... :..
Oxen ....
Cows ....
Calves ....

CERTIFICATE BY CONSULAR OFFICER.

I, C. D., vice-consul [*or as the case may be*] of Her Britannic Majesty at the port of Husum [*or as the case may be*], hereby certify that the foregoing declaration was made by the above-named A. B. before me, this —— day of ——, 1873, and that I know the said A. B., and that he is worthy of belief.

(To be signed.)   C. D.
[and consular seal to be affixed.]

----

* Number to be expressed in words and figures.

CERTIFICATE OF OFFICER OF ROYAL PRUSSIAN PROVINCIAL COUNCIL OFFICE.

I, X. Y., hereby certify that I have this day seen the cattle above described, and that I believe the statement respecting the breeding and feeding of each of them contained in the foregoing declaration of A. B. to be true in all respects.

(To be signed.)
                                                      X. Y.

Office of Royal Prussian Provincial Council Office at the Port of Husem [or as the case may be].

28. With respect to the metropolis, notwithstanding anything in this act or in the second schedule thereto, the following provisions shall have effect :

(1.) The mayor, aldermen, and commons of the city of London shall, for the purposes of this part of this act, be exclusively the local authority in and for the metropolis.

(2.) The mayor, aldermen, and commons, on exercising for the purposes of this part of this act the borrowing powers vested in a local authority under this act, may borrow on the credit of the property on the credit whereof they are authorized to borrow by the metropolitan market act, 1865, and the money so borrowed may be secured in the manner and subject and according to the provisions in that act authorized and contained.

(3.) All money received by the mayor, aldermen, and commons from charges made by them under this part of this act shall (subject to the application thereof as in this part of this act directed in payment of interest on and in repayment of principal of money borrowed for the purposes of this part of this act) be applied in repayment of the principal of money borrowed by them under the metropolitan market acts, 1857 and 1865, and subject thereto in discharge of expenses incurred by them in the execution of this part of this act.

(4.) From and after the opening for public use of a market provided by the mayor, aldermen, and commons under this part of this act to the satisfaction of the privy council (declared by order), the maximum tolls, dues, and payments that may be taken under the metropolitan market act, 1857, in respect of the animals mentioned in the fifth schedule to this act, shall be the sums in that schedule specified in lieu of those specified in schedule A to that act.

29. Provided that if the mayor, aldermen, and commons of the city of London do not before the first day of January, one thousand eight hundred and seventy-two, provide and open for public use a market for the purposes of this part of this act to the satisfaction of the privy council (declared by order), then on and after that day the following consequences shall ensue :

(1.) The provision of this part of this act making the mayor; aldermen, and commons exclusively for the purposes of this part of this act the local authority in and for the metropolis shall cease to operate.

(2.) The enactment in section 15 of the metropolitan market act, 1857, that no new market for the sale of cattle or horses shall be opened in the cities of London or Westminster, or the liberties thereof, or in the borough of Southwark, or at any place distant less than seven miles in a straight line from St. Paul's Cathedral, in the city of London, shall not prevent any local authority or person from establishing a market for the purposes of this part of this act in or at any place named or defined in that section.

30. Where a local authority, with the approval of the privy council, have, before or after the passing of this act provided, erected, and fitted up within a part of a port defined by the privy council as a place where foreign animals may be landed any wharf, lair, shed, market, house, or place for the landing, reception, sale, or slaughter of foreign animals, it shall not be lawful for the privy council (as long as importation of foreign animals for that port is allowed, but under restriction) to revoke the definition of the part or parts of that port at which foreign animals may be landed, or to alter it so as to exclude therefrom any part of the site of such wharf, lair, shed, market, house, or place, except with the consent of the local authority; and if any railway company have provided, erected, or fitted up any such wharves, lairs, sheds, markets, houses, or places, the same may, with the approval of the privy council, be used for the purposes of this part of this act.

(By an order in council (341) of December 20, 1871, the restrictions imposed by the metropolitan contagious diseases (animals) order of August, 1869, were revoked after December 31st of that year.)

PART IV.—DISCOVERY AND PREVENTION OF DISEASE.

31. An inspector of a local authority, on receiving information of the supposed existence of cattle-plague, pleuro-pneumonia, or sheep-pox, or having reasonable ground to suspect that any of those diseases existed in any place within his district, shall

proceed to that place with all practical speed, and execute and discharge the powers and duties by or under this act conferred and imposed on him as inspector.

32. An inspector or other officer of a local authority, authorized to act in the execution of this act, may at any time enter any field, stable, cow-shed, or other premises within his district where he has reasonable grounds for supposing that any animal affected with cattle-plague, pleuro-pneumonia, or sheep-pox is to be found, for the purpose of executing this act, but shall, if required, state in writing the grounds on which he has so entered.

If any person refuses admission to such inspector or officer acting under this section, he shall be deemed guilty of an offense against this act.

33. The certificate of an inspector of a local authority to the effect that an animal within his district is affected with cattle-plague, pleuro-pneumonia, or sheep-pox shall for the purposes of this act be conclusive evidence in all courts of justice and elsewhere of the matter certified.

Infected places : cattle-plague and sheep-pox.

34. Where an inspector finds cattle-plague or sheep-pox to exist within his district, he shall forthwith make a declaration thereof under his hand, and shall deliver a notice under his hand of such declaration to the occupier of the field, stable, cow-shed, or other premises where the disease is found, and thereupon the same, with all lands and buildings contiguous thereto in the same occupation, shall become and be an infected place, and the same shall continue to be an infected place until the determination and declaration of the local authority relative thereto in this act provided for.

35. Where an inspector makes such a declaration of the existence of cattle-plague or sheep-pox, he shall with all practicable speed send a copy thereof to the privy council, and deliver the declaration to the local authority, who shall forthwith inquire into the correctness thereof, and if it appears to them that cattle-plague or sheep-pox existed as declared by the inspector, they shall so determine and declare, and shall prescribe the limits of the infected place; but if it appears to them that cattle-plague or sheep-pox did not exist as declared by the inspector, and the same is certified to them in writing by one or more duly qualified veterinary surgeon or surgeons, employed by them in that behalf, they shall so determine and declare, and thereupon the place comprised in the inspector's declaration, or affected thereby, shall cease to be an infected place.

36. A local authority, with respect to any place within their district, and the privy council, with respect to any place in Great Britain, may from time to time by order declare any field, stable, cow-shed, or other premises in which cattle-plague or sheep-pox exists at the date of the order, or has existed within seven days before that date, with or without a further area, to be from and after a time specified in the order an infected place.

37. The area of an infected place may in all cases of a declaration by a local authority include, with the field, stable, cow-shed, or other premises in which cattle-plague or sheep-pox has been found to exist, all lands and buildings lying contiguous thereto, being in the same occupation, and within the district of the local authority, and also (except in the metropolis) an area comprised within one mile from the boundaries of those lands in every direction, but no more.

38. A local authority may include in the area of an infected place any adjoining part of the district of another local authority, with the previous consent of that authority in writing signed by their clerk, but not otherwise.

39. The area of an infected place may in all cases of a declaration by the privy council include, with the field, stable, cow-shed, or other premises in which cattle-plague or sheep-pox has been found to exist, such an area as to the privy council seems to be requisite.

40. With respect to the metropolis, the privy council may from time to time, by order, extend the limits of an infected place beyond the boundaries of the field, stable, cow-shed, farm, or premises where cattle-plague or sheep-pox is declared or found to exist.

41. The area of an infected place may in any case be described by reference to a map deposited at some specified place, or by reference to townships, parishes, farms, or otherwise.

42. An order of a local authority declaring a place to be an infected place shall be published by the local authority by notices posted in and near the infected place, and in such other manner (if any) as they think expedient.

An order of the privy council declaring a place to be an infected place shall be published in like manner by and at the expense of any local authority to whom the same is sent by the privy council for publication.

Any want of or defect or irregularity in publication shall not invalidate any order.

43. An order of a local authority or of the privy council declaring a place to be an infected place shall be conclusive evidence in all courts of justice and elsewhere of the existence of disease and other matters on which the order proceeds.

44. The rules set forth in the sixth schedule to this act shall have effect with respect to infected places (which rules are in this act referred to as the rules of this act with respect to infected places).

45. If any animal, hide, skin, hair, wool, horn, hoof, offal, carcass, meat, dung, hay, straw, litter, or other thing is moved in contravention of the rules of this act with respect to infected places, every person moving the same or causing the same to be moved shall be deemed guilty of an offense against this act.

46. The rules of this act with respect to infected places shall not restrict the moving of any animal or thing by railway through an infected place, such animal or thing not being stopped within the infected place.

47. The privy council may from time to time by order make rules with respect to infected places, not being inconsistent with the rules set forth in the sixth schedule to this act; and with respect to the metropolis the privy council thereunder relative to infected to time, if they think it expedient, vary the rules set forth in that schedule; and all rules and variations of rules so made shall be deemed rules of this act with respect to infected places.

48. Every local authority and the police of every county, borough, town, and place shall, within their respective districts, enforce and execute the provisions of this act and of any order of the local authority or privy council thereunder relative to infected places, and do or cause to be done all things from time to time necessary or expedient for securing as far as may be the effectual isolation of infected places in respect of the movement of animals and things.

49. Any constable may proceed as follows :

(1.) He may apprehend any person found committing an offense against the rules of this act with respect to infected places, and he shall take any person so apprehended, as soon as conveniently may be, before a justice of the peace, to be examined and dealt with according to law; and a person so apprehended shall not be detained in custody by any constable without the order of a justice longer than is necessary for bringing him before a justice, or than twenty-four hours at longest.

(2.) He may require that any animal or thing moved out of an infected place in contravention of those rules be forthwith taken back within the limits of that place, and may enforce and execute such requisition.

50. The local authority by whom an infected place is declared may at any time after the expiration of twenty-eight days from the disappearance of cattle-plague or sheep-pox (as the case may be) in that place, by order declare the place to be free from cattle-plague or sheep-pox (as the case may be).

The privy council may at any time by order declare any place to be free from cattle-plague or sheep-pox.

Thereupon, as from the time specified in this behalf in the order of the local authority or privy council, the place shall cease to be an infected place as regards cattle-plague or sheep-pox (as the case may be).

51. The clerk of a local authority declaring a place to be an infected place, or declaring a place to be free from cattle-plague or sheep-pox, shall forthwith report by post to the privy council the fact of such declaration having been made.

52. An order of the privy council relative to an infected place shall supersede any order of a local authority inconsistent with it.

53. Where, under this act, an inspector makes a declaration which constitutes a place an infected place, he may also, if the circumstances of the case appear to him so to require, deliver a notice under his hand of such declaration to the occupiers of all lands and buildings adjoining thereto, any part whereof respectively lies within one mile of the boundaries of the infected place in any direction, and thereupon the rules of this act with respect to infected places shall, until the determination and declaration of the local authority relative thereto in this act provided for, apply and have effect to and in respect of those lands and buildings as if the same were actually within the limits of the infected place.

Pleuro-pneumonia.

54. Where an inspector finds pleuro-pneumonia to exist within his district, he shall forthwith make a declaration thereof under his hand, and shall deliver a notice under his hand of such declaration to the occupier of the field, stable, cow-shed, or other premises where the disease is found; and thereupon the rules set forth in the seventh schedule to this act (in this act called the pleuro-pneumonia rules of this act) shall have effect in relation to such field, stable, cow-shed, or other premises, until the determination and declaration of the local authority relative thereto in this act provided for.

55. Where an inspector makes a declaration of the existence of pleuro-pneumonia, he shall with all practicable speed send a copy thereof to the privy council, and deliver the declaration to the local authority, who shall inquire into the correctness thereof; and if it appears to them that pleuro-pneumonia existed as declared by the inspector, they shall so determine and declare, and thereupon the pleuro-pneumonia rules of this act shall continue to apply to the field, stable, cow-shed, or other premises

to which the declaration relates ; but if in any such case it appears to the local authority that pleuro-pneumonia did not exist as declared by the inspector, or that a fresh case of pleuro-pneumonia has not occurred for thirty days in such field, stable, cowshed, or other premises, then the local authority shall so determine and declare, and the pleuro-pneumonia rules of this act shall cease to operate in relation thereto.

Miscellaneous.

56. The forms given in the eighth schedule to this act, with such variations as circumstances require, may be used by an inspector for the purposes of this part of this act, and a declaration of disease under this part of this act shall not be deemed a certificate of the inspector for any purpose of this act.

57. If any person exposes in a market or fair or other public place where horses or animals are commonly exposed for sale, or exposes for sale in any sale-yard, whether public or private, or places in a lair or other place adjacent to or connected with a market or fair, or where horses or animals are commonly placed before exposure for sale, or sends or causes to be carried on a railway or on a canal, river, or other inland navigation, or on a coasting vessel, or carries, leads, or drives, or causes to be carried, led, or driven on a highway or thoroughfare any horse or animal affected with a contagious or infectious disease, he shall be deemed guilty of an offense against this act, unless he shows to the satisfaction of the justices before whom he is charged that he did not know of the same being so affected, and that he could not with reasonable diligence have obtained such knowledge.

Where any horse or animal so affected is exposed or otherwise dealt with in contravention of this section an inspection of the local authority or any officer of the local authority authorized to act in execution of this act may seize the same and cause it, if affected with glanders, cattle-plague, or sheep-pox, to be slaughtered, and if affected with any other contagious or infectious disease to be removed to some convenient or isolated place and to be there kept for such time as the local authority think expedient, and the local authority may recover the expenses of the execution by them of this section from the owner of the horse or animal, or from the consignor or cousignee thereof, who may recover the same from the owner.

In case of a conviction of an offense under this section no compensation shall be payable in respect of any animals slaughtered under this section.

Notwithstanding anything in this section, the privy council may from time to time, by order, make such further or other provision as they think expedient respecting animals becoming affected with foot-and-mouth disease or any other contagious or infectious disease not being cattle-plague, pleuro-pneumonia, sheep-pox, or glanders while exposed or placed or being carried, led, or driven as aforesaid, and any such order shall be deemed part of this section.

An order of council (355) dated August 8, 1872, refers to the cleansing and disinfection of markets, &c., in the following terms :

1. This order may be cited as the market order of 1872.
2. This order extends to Great Britain only.
3. Words in this order have the same meaning as in the act of 1869.
4. Every local authority is hereby empowered to make from time to time, with the view of preventing the spreading of contagious or infectious disease among animals, regulations for the following purposes, or any of them :

(1.) For requiring the owners, lessees, or occupiers of places used for the holding of markets, fairs, exhibitions, or sales of animals, or for the lairage of animals, to cleanse those places from time to time at their own expense.

(2.) For requiring the owners, lessees, or occupiers of those places to disinfect the same, or any specified part thereof, from time to time at their own expense, where, in the judgment of the local authority, the circumstances are such as to allow of such disinfection being reasonably required.

(3.) For prescribing the mode in which such cleaning and such disinfection shall be effected.

5. Notwithstanding anything in the animals order of 1871, article 39 of that order shall not apply to the cleansing and disinfecting of any such place as aforesaid.

6. If the owner, lessee, or occupier of any such place as aforesaid does any act in contravention of the regulations of a local authority under this order, or fails in respect to observe the same, it shall not be lawful for him or any other person at any time thereafter, until further order of the privy council, to hold a market, fair, exhibition, or sale of animals in that place, and the holding therein of any market, fair, exhibition, or sale of animals shall be and the same is hereby prohibited accordingly, and if any person holds any market, fair, exhibition, or sale of animals in contravention of this order, shall be deemed guilty of an offense against this order.

58. If any person places or keeps on any common or uninclosed land or in any field or other place insufficiently fenced, or on the side of a highway, any horse or animal

affected with a contagious or infectious disease, he shall be deemed guilty of an offense against this act, unless he shows to the satisfaction of the justices before whom he is charged that he did not know of the same being so affected, and that he could not with reasonable diligence have obtained such knowledge.

59. Where a person having cattle in his possession or keeping within the district of a local authority wherein cattle plague exists affixes at the entrance to a building or inclosed place in or on which such cattle are kept a notice forbidding persons to enter into or on that building or place without his permission, then, if any person not having a right of entry or way into, on, or over that building or place, enters into, on, or over the same or any part thereof, in contravention of the notice he shall for every such offense be liable to a penalty not exceeding five pounds.

60. Every local authority shall cause every horse or animal that has died of glanders, cattle plague, or sheep-pox, or has been slaughtered in consequence of being affected with glanders, cattle plague, or sheep-pox, within their district to be buried as soon as possible in its skin in some proper place, and to be covered with a sufficient quantity of quicklime or other disinfectant, and with not less than six feet of earth, or to be destroyed under inspection of the local authority in such mode as the privy council may from time to time by order direct or approve.

It shall not be lawful for any person, except with the license of the privy council, to dig up or cause to be dug up the carcass or any part of the carcass of any horse or animal so buried.

An order of council (341), dated December 20, 1871, thus amends and renews the regulations relating to contagious or infectious disease among animals:

Discovery and prevention of disease.

19. Every person having in his possession or under his charge an animal (including a horse) affected with a contagious or infectious disease shall observe the following rules:

(1.) He shall, as far as practicable, keep such animal separate from animals not so affected.

(2.) He shall with all practicable speed give notice to a police constable of the fact of the animal being so affected.

Such police constable shall forthwith give notice thereof to the inspector of the local authority, and (except in the case of foot-and-mouth disease) to the privy council.

20. Where an inspector finds in his district cattle plague, pleuro-pneumonia, sheeppox, sheep-scab, or glanders, he shall forthwith make a return thereof to the local authority and to the privy council, on a form provided by the privy council, with all particulars therein required, and shall continue to make a similar return on the Saturday of every week until the disease has disappeared.

21. Any dung of animals, and any hay, straw, litter, or other thing, commonly used for food of animals or otherwise for or about animals, may be moved out of an infected place within the metropolis (but not out of the metropolis) with a license signed by an officer of the local authority appointed on that behalf, certifying that the thing moved has been disinfected, but not otherwise.

22. Any officer authorized in this behalf by a local authority, or any constable or police officer, may stop and detain any animal (including a horse) which is being moved, or which he has reasonable grounds for suspecting is being moved, in contravention of the act of 1869 or any order of council, and may apprehend, without warrant, the person in charge thereof, and bring him before a justice, who shall inquire into the case in a summary manner, and may, if satisfied that there are good grounds for so suspecting, by writing under his hand, direct the animal to be detained, and the person in charge thereof to be brought before two justices as soon as practicable.

On such person being brought before two justices, they shall adjudicate on the case in a summary manner, and if satisfied that the animal was being moved in contravention, as aforesaid, may direct it to be disposed of in conformity with the provisions of the act of 1869 or any order of council.

23. Any officer authorized in this behalf by a local authority, or any constable or police officer, may inspect any railway truck, cart, boat, or other vehicle used by land or by water, in which animals, including horses, hay, manure, litter, straw, and other articles used for or about animals are usually or at the time of such inspection carried, and may examine the person in charge thereof with a view to ascertain whether any animals or articles are being moved or carried in contravention of the act of 1869 or any order of council; and such officer may, if he has reasonable grounds for suspecting that such animals or articles are being moved or carried in contravention as aforesaid, apprehend, without warrant, the person in charge thereof, and bring him before a justice, who shall inquire into the case in a summary manner, and may, if satisfied that there are good grounds for so suspecting, by writing under his hand, direct the same to be obtained, and the person in charge thereof to be brought before two justices as soon as practicable.

On such person being brought before two justices, they shall adjudicate on the case in a summary manner, and if satisfied that the animals or articles were being moved or carried in contravention as aforesaid, may direct the same to be destroyed or otherwise disposed of in conformity with the provisions of the act of 1869 or any order of council.

24. Any person having charge of any animal (including a horse), or thing that is being moved on a highway, railway, canal, navigation, or river, for the moving whereof a license is requisite, shall, on being so required by an officer of a local authority authorized in this behalf, or by a constable or police officer, produce the license (if any) for the moving of that animal or thing.

25. A constable or police or other officer, detaining any animal (including a horse) under the act of 1869 or any order of council, shall cause it to be supplied with requisite food and water during its detention ; and any expenses incurred by him in respect thereof may be recovered from the person in charge of the animal or from its owner.

26. Any inspector or other officer empowered to carry the act of 1869 or any order of council into effect may, if authorized in this behalf by general or special order in writing of the local authority, enter, for the purpose of carrying into effect, the provisions of such act or order, any field, stable, cow-shed, or other premises within his district, where he has reasonable grounds for supposing that any animal affected with cattle-plague or sheep-pox has been, or has been buried or otherwise disposed of.

If any person refuses admission to or obstructs or impedes, or aids in obstructing or impeding, such inspector or other officer, he shall be deemed guilty of an offence against this order.

27. A local authority may, from time to time, with the view of preventing the spreading of contagious or infectious disease, make regulations for the following purposes or any of them.

For prohibiting or regulating the movement of animals (including horses) on, to, from, and through, and the keeping thereof on commons and wastes and commonable and other lands whereon there exists a right of common or other right in the nature thereof.

For preventing any person from driving animals (including horses) under his charge, or allowing them to be driven or to stray into an inclosed field or place without the consent of the occupier thereof.

For preventing the spreading by means of dogs of any such disease.

For prohibiting or regulating the removal of hay, straw, litter, or other thing commonly used for food of animals, or otherwise for or about animals, that has been in the same field, stable, cow-shed, or other premises with animals affected with any contagious or infectious disease, or any dung that has been therein.

For providing for the cleansing and disinfection of sheds and places used by animals affected with any contagious or infectious disease.

Foot-and-mouth disease.

28. A local authority may, from time to time, with the view of preventing the spreading of foot-and-mouth disease, make regulations for the following purposes, or any of them :

For prohibiting or regulating the movement out of any field, stable, cow-shed, or other premises in which foot-and-mouth disease has been found to exist, of any animal, that has been in the same field, stable, cow-shed, or other premises with or in contact with any animal affected with foot-and-mouth disease.

Sheep-scab.

29. A local authority may, from time to time, with the view of preventing the spreading of sheep-scab, make regulations for the following purposes, or any of them :

For prohibiting any person from having in his possession or under his charge a sheep affected with sheep-scab, without treating that sheep, or causing it to be treated, with some dressing or dipping or other remedy for sheep-scab.

For prohibiting or regulating the movement out of any field, stable, cow-shed, or other premises, in which sheep-scab has been found to exist, of any sheep that has been in contact with, or in the same field, stable, cow-shed, or other premises, with any sheep affected with sheep-scab.

Pleuro-pneumonia.

30. A local authority may, from time to time, with the view of preventing the spreading of pleuro-pneumonia, make regulations for the following purposes, or any of them :

For prohibiting or regulating the removal out of any field, stable, cow-shed, or other premises, of the carcasses of any cattle which have died or have been slaughtered in consequence of being affected with pleuro-pneumonia.

Provided, that such local authority shall, from time to time, define the area within their district within which any such regulation shall have effect.

31. Where a local authority is authorized by the privy council to slaughter cattle affected with pleuro-pneumonia, such local authority may cause all cattle affected with pleuro-pneumonia within their district to be slaughtered, subject to the following provisions:

(1.) The local authority shall, by way of compensation for every such animal, pay to the owner thereof such sum, not exceeding one-half of the value of the animal immediately before it was affected with pleuro-pneumonia, as to the local authority seem fit.

(2.) They may require the value of any such animal to be ascertained by their officers, or by arbitration, and generally they may impose conditions as to evidence of the slaughter and value of any such animal.

(3.) They may, if they think fit, withhold compensation in respect of any such animal where the owner or the person having the charge thereof has, in their judgment, been guilty, in relation to such animal, of any act in contravention of the act of 1869 or of any order or regulation or license of the privy council or of a local authority, or has, in relation to such animal, failed to comply with the provisions of the act of 1869 or of any such order, regulation, or license in respect of the giving of notice of disease, or in any other respect.

32. The expenditure of a local authority in pursuance of this order in respect of compensation for cattle slaughtered as being affected with pleuro-pneumonia, shall be defrayed out of the local rate.

33. Where the local authority in pursuance of this order causes any animal to be slaughtered as affected with pleuro-pneumonia, the owner thereof shall not be entitled to recover in respect of the insurance thereof any sum, which, together with the payment which he receives for the same under this order, would exceed the sum which he would have been entitled to receive in respect of the insurance.

34. Every local authority shall keep, in such manner and form as the privy council from time to time direct or approve, a record, stating the date of any order made by them for slaughter under this order, and the execution of the order, and other proper particulars, and such record shall be evidence if any question arises concerning an order for the slaughter of any such animal or concerning compensation in respect thereof.

35. Where a local authority is authorized by the privy council to put in operation this provision of this order, such local authority may, from time to time, with the view of preventing the spreading of pleuro-pneumonia, prohibit or regulate the holding of any specified market, fair, auction, sale, or exhibition of cattle within their district.

An order of council (366) dated August 2, 1873, is important with regard to contagious pleuro-pneumonia and foot-and-mouth disease. It is as follows:

1. This order may be cited as the the animals' (amendment) order of 1873.

2. This order shall take effect from and immediately after the thirty-first day of August, one thousand eight hundred and seventy-three, and words in this order have the same meaning as in the act of 1869.

Pleuro-pneumonia.

3. Every local authority shall cause all cattle affected with pleuro-pneumonia within their district to be slaughtered.

The provisions numbered 1, 2, and 3, of article 31, and articles 32, 33, and 34, relating to compensation of the animals order of 1871, shall have effect in case of slaughter under this article of this order.

Foot-and-mouth disease.

4. Foot-and-mouth disease shall not be deemed to be a contagious or infectious disease within either of the following articles of the animals order of 1871, namely, articles 19 and 27.

Any regulations made by a local authority under the said article 27, as far as they relate to foot-and-mouth disease, are hereby revoked.

5. Where an animal becomes affected with foot-and-mouth disease while exposed or placed or being carried, led, or driven, as in section 57 of the act of 1869 mentioned, it may, notwithstanding anything in that section, be, with a license of an inspector of the local authority authorized to issue the same, but not otherwise, moved for purposes of feeding, or watering, or other ordinary purposes connected with the breeding or rearing of animals, to any land or building in the occupation of the owner of the animal, or for slaughter to the nearest slaughter house, or some other slaughter house approved by the local authority.

The form given in the second schedule to this order, or a form to the like effect, with such variations as circumstances require, shall be used.

Revocation.

6. The order and part of an order of council described in the first schedule to this order, and any regulations made by a local authority under that part of an order, are hereby revoked; provided that nothing in this order shall invalidate or make unlawful anything done under the said orders and part of an order and regulations, or interfere with the institution or prosecution of any proceeding in respect of any offense committed against, or any penalty or forfeiture incurred under, the same.

An order in council, issued in June, 1874, revokes article 5 of the above; consequently articles 19, 27, and 28, of the animals (amendment) order of 1873, are restored.

Burial and disinfection.

36. Where, under section 60 of the act of 1869, a horse or animal is buried, its skin shall be first so slashed as to prevent its being of any use. The local authorities may, if they think fit, use for the purpose of such burial any place on the premises of the owner of the horse or animal.

37. Where a local authority is authorized by license from the privy council to destroy, under section 60 of the act of 1869, horses or animals that have died or been slaughtered as therein mentioned, every such horse or animal shall be destroyed in manner following, namely: The carcass thereof shall be disinfected, and shall then be removed, in charge of an officer of the local authority, to a horse slaughterer's or knacker's yard, licensed for the purpose by the privy council, or other place so licensed, and shall be there destroyed by exposure to a high temperature, or by chemical agents. In every such case the local authority shall report to the privy council the fact and mode of destruction.

38. Where a local authority exercise the power of causing premises to be cleansed and disinfected, conferred on them by the act of 1869, or by any order of council, the occupier of those premises shall give all facilities for that purpose.

39. Where any landing-place, lair, shed, or other place, is directed by the act of 1869, or any order of council, or is ordered by a local authority, to be cleansed and disinfected, it shall be cleansed and disinfected in manner following:

(1.) By the sweeping out thereof, and the effectual removal therefrom of all dung, sawdust, litter, and other matter.

(2.) Then by thorough washing therewith with water.

(3.) Then by the application to the floor and to all parts above the floor with which animals or their droppings have come in contact, of a coating of lime, made by mixing good freshly-burnt lime with water, and containing in each gallon of lime-wash either one-fifth of a pint of commercial carbolic acid, or one-fifth of a pint of commercial cresylic acid, or four ounces of fresh dry chloride of lime, such lime-wash to be prepared immediately before use.

The sweepings of the landing place, lair, shed, or other place, shall be well mixed with quicklime, and effectually removed from contact with animals.

General provisions.

40. A local authority may from time to time revoke or alter any order, prohibition, or regulation made by them under the act of 1869 or any order of council.

41. Every local authority shall send to the privy council a copy of every order, prohibition, or regulation made by them.

42. If the privy council are satisfied on inquiry with respect to any prohibition or regulation made by a local authority under the act of 1869, or any order of council, that the same is of too restrictive a character, or otherwise objectionable, and direct the revocation thereof, the same shall thereupon cease to operate.

43. Whenever there is any change in the name or address of any inspector appointed under section 12 of the act of 1869, or in the district of any such inspector, the local authority shall forthwith report the same to the privy council.

44. Except where otherwise provided for in any order of council, a local authority shall provide and supply, without charge, printed copies of documents or forms requisite under the act of 1869 or any order of council.

45. Every regulation made by a local authority under any order of council shall (where no other provision is made for the publication thereof) be published by advertisement in a newspaper circulating in the district of the local authority.

46. If any person fails to give, produce, do, or observe any notice, license, thing, or rule which he is by this order or by any order or regulation of a local authority thereunder required to give, produce, do, or observe, he shall in every such case be deemed guilty of an offense against this order.

47. If any animal (including a horse) or anything is moved or dealt with in contravention of this order or of any order or regulation of a local authority thereunder, the owner thereof and the person directing or permitting such movement thereof or deal-

ing therewith, and the person or company in charge of or removing or conveying the same, shall each be deemed guilty of an offense against this order.

48. All orders and regulations made by a local authority under any former order of council and in force at the commencement of this order shall, as far as the same are not varied by or inconsistent with this order, remain in force until altered or revoked by the local authority.

61. A local authority shall cause the yard, shed, stable, field, or other premises in which any horse or animal affected with glanders or cattle plague or sheep-pox has been kept while so affected, or has died or been slaughtered, to be thoroughly cleansed and disinfected, and all hay, straw, litter, dung, or other article that has been in contact with or used about any such horse or animal to be burned or otherwise destroyed.

No fresh animal shall be admitted into any yard, shed, stable, field, or other premises in which any animal affected with cattle plague or sheep-pox has been kept while so affected, or has died or been slaughtered, until the expiration of thirty days after the cleansing and disinfecting of such premises in pursuance of this act.

Any such hay, straw, litter, dung, or other article shall not be removed from the premises in which any horse or animal affected with glanders or cattle plague has been, except for the purpose of being destroyed, nor shall it be removed out of the district of the local authority without the consent in writing of the local authority into whose district it is moved. If any such thing is removed in contravention of this act, the occupier of the premises from which it is removed and the person removing it shall be deemed guilty of an offense against this act.

A local authority shall direct the disinfecting of the clothes of, and the use of due precautions against the spreading of contagion by, inspectors and others in contact with animals affected with cattle plague.

62. Every steamboat, railway, and other public company, and every person carrying animals for hire to or in Great Britain, shall thoroughly cleanse and disinfect, in such manner as the privy council from time to time by order direct, all steamers, vessels, boats, pens, carriages, trucks, horse-boxes, and vehicles used by such company or person for the carrying of animals.

If any company or person on any occasion fails to comply with the requisitions of any such order, such company or person shall on every such occasion be deemed guilty of an offense against this act.

An inspector of a local authority or any officer of a local authority authorized to execute this act, may at all times enter on board any steamer, vessel, or boat in respect whereof he has reasonable grounds for supposing that any company or person has failed to comply with the requisitions of any such order, and on premises where he has reasonable grounds for supposing that any pen, carriage, truck, horse-box, or vehicle in respect whereof any company or person has on any occasion so failed is to be found ; and if any company or person refuses admission to an inspector or other officer acting under this section, such company or person shall be deemed guilty of an offense against this act.

63. The privy council may from time to time, by order, give directions respecting modes of disinfecting, and anything disinfected in accordance with the provisions of such order, or in accordance with any process of disinfection approved by the privy council shall be deemed disinfected within this act, but not otherwise.

63. Every railway company shall make a provision to the satisfaction of the privy council, of water and food, or either of them, at such stations as the privy council from time to time by general or specific description direct, for animals carried or about to be, or having been, carried on the railway of the company ; and such water and food, or either of them, shall be supplied to any such animal by the company carrying it on the request in writing of the consignor thereof, or on the request of any person in charge thereof, and the company so supplying water and food, or either of them, may make in respect thereof such reasonable charges, if any, as the privy council by order approve, in addition to such charges as they are for the time being authorized to make in respect of the carriage of animals, and the amount of such additional charges accrued due in respect of any animal shall be a debt from the consignor and from the consignee thereof to the company, and shall be recoverable by the company from either of them by proceedings in any court of competent jurisdiction, and the company shall have a lien for the amount thereof, on the animal in respect of which the same accrued due, and on any other animal at any time consigned by the same person to be carried by the company.

If any company on any occasion fails to comply with the requirements of this section they shall on every such occasion be deemed guilty of an offense against this act. If in the case of any animal such a request as aforesaid is not made so that the animal remains without a supply of water for thirty consecutive hours, or other period not being less than twelve hours, as the privy council from time to time by order prescribe, the consignor and the person in charge of the animal shall each be deemed guilty of an offense against this act; and it shall lie on the person accused to prove the time within which the animal has had a supply of water.

By an order of council (341) dated December 20, 1871, the following renewed and amended regulations with regard to transit are made :

Transit of animals by sea.

5. In this part of this order the term "animals" extends to all ruminating animals and to horses.

6. With respect to places used for animals on board vessels, the following regulations shall have effect :

(1.) Every such place shall be divided into pens by substantial divisions.

(2.) Each pen shall not exceed 9 feet in breadth, or 15 feet in length.

(3.) The floor of each pen shall have proper battens or other foot-holds thereon.

(4.) Every such place, if inclosed, shall be ventilated by means of separate inlet and outlet openings, of such size and position as will secure a proper supply of air to the place in all states of weather.

7. Between each first day of November and the following thirtieth day of April (both days inclusive) freshly-shorn sheep shall not be carried on the deck of a vessel.

8. When sheep are carried on the deck of a vessel, proper gangways shall be provided either between or above the pens in which the sheep are carried.

9. Animals landed from a vessel shall, on a certificate of an inspector appointed by the privy council in that behalf, certifying to the effect that the foregoing regulations, or some one of them, have not or has not been observed in the vessel, be detained at the landing place or in lairs adjacent thereto, until the privy council otherwise direct.

Cleansing and disinfection of vessels.

10. Every vessel used for carrying animals shall, after the close of each voyage, and before any fresh cargo is put on board, be cleansed and disinfected in manner following :

(1.) By the sweeping out of the hold and every other part of the vessel used for animals, and the actual removal therefrom of all dung and litter, and of all ashes, sand, sawdust, and other matter with which animals or their droppings have come in contact.

(2.) Then by the thorough washing of the same parts of the vessel with water.

(3.) Then by the application to the sides, floor, and ceiling of the hold and to every other part of the vessel with which animals or their droppings have come in contact, of a coating of limewash made by mixing good, freshly burnt lime with water, and containing in each gallon of limewash either one-fifth of a pint of commercial carbolic acid, or one-fifth of a pint of commercial cresylic acid, or four ounces of fresh dry chloride of lime, such limewash to be prepared immediately before use.

The sweepings of the vessel shall be well mixed with quicklime, and effectually removed from contact with animals.

Shipping and unshipping places.

11. At every place where animals are put on board of or landed from vessels, provision shall be made, to the satisfaction of the privy council, for a supply of water for animals, and water shall be supplied there, gratuitously, on request of any person in charge of any animals.

12. At every place where animals are landed from vessels, provision shall be made, to the satisfaction of the privy council, for the speedy and convenient unshipment of animals, and for a supply of food for them ; and food shall be supplied there, on request of any person in charge of any animals, at such price as the privy council from time to time approve.

Cleansing and disinfection of landing-places.

13. Where any animal affected with any contagious or infectious disease is landed at a port, or is, while so affected, in or at any landing-place or lair, or other place adjacent thereto, then the landing-place and every such lair or other place where the animal has been shall not be used for any animals not forming part of the same cargo unless and until it has been cleansed and disinfected.

Transit of animals by railway.

14. Every truck used for carrying animals on a railway shall be provided with spring buffers, and the floor thereof shall have proper battens or other foothold thereon.

15. A railway company shall not allow any truck used for carrying animals on their railway to be overcrowded so as to cause unnecessary suffering to the animals therein.

16. Between each 1st day of November and the next following 30th day of April (both days inclusive), trucks used for carrying on a railway sheep freshly shorn and unclothed shall be covered and inclosed so as to protect the sheep from the weather, but shall be properly ventilated.

Cleansing and disinfection of pens and vehicles.

17. Every pen, carriage, truck, horse-box, or vehicle used for carrying animals on land, shall, on every occasion after any animal is taken out of the same, and before any other animal is placed therein, be cleansed and disinfected in manner following :

(1.) By the sweeping out of the pen, carriage, truck, horse-box, or vehicle, and the effectual removal therefrom of all dung, sawdust, litter, and other matter.

(2.) Then by the thorough washing of the pen, carriage, truck, horse-box, or vehicle with water.

(3.) Then, in case of a pen, carriage, or truck, by the application to the floor and to all parts above the floor with which animals or their droppings have come in contact, of a coating of limewash, made by mixing good, freshly-burnt lime with water, and containing in each gallon of limewash either one-fifth of a pint of commercial carbolic acid, or one-fifth of a pint of commercial cresylic acid, or four ounces of fresh, dry chloride of lime, such limewash to be prepared immediately before use.

The sweepings of the pen, carriage, truck, horse-box, or vehicle shall be well mixed with quicklime and carefully removed from contact with animals.

PENALTIES.

18. If anything is done or omitted to be done in contravention of any of the regulations of this part of this order, the owner and the master or person having charge or command of the vessel in which ; and the owner and the occupier of the place where animals are put on board of or landed from vessels at which ; and the company carrying animals on or owning or working a railway on which ; and also in case of the overcrowding of a truck on a railway, or of the carrying on a railway of sheep freshly shorn and unclothed, the consignor of the animals in respect of which (as the case may be), such thing is done or omitted, shall severally be deemed guilty of an offense against this order.

Provided, that no person shall be liable to a penalty under this part of this order in respect of sheep as freshly shorn, where it is proved that the sheep have not been shorn within sixty days before the time of the commission of the alleged offense.

By an order in council (349) dated July 11, 1872, the following regulation was to take effect from July 3 (1) of that year :

(2.) This order may be cited as the carcasses of animals' order of 1872.

(3.) In this order—
The act of 1869 means the contagious diseases (animals') act, 1869.
Master includes any person having the charge or command of a vessel.
Other terms have the same meaning as in the act of 1869.

4. In addition to the powers and duties vested in and imposed on local authorities by section sixty of the act of 1869, and by articles 36 and 37 of the animals order of 1871, every local authority is hereby empowered to make, from time to time, with the view of preventing the spreading of contagious or infectious diseases among animals, regulations for the following purpose :

For securing the burial, in accordance with the directions of article 36 of the Animals order of 1871, of the carcasses, being within the district of the local authority of animals (including horses) which have died of any contagious or infectious disease, or the destruction thereof, under inspection of the local authority, in the mode prescribed by article 37 of the animals order of 1871.

5. If an animal (including a horse) on board a vessel in Great Britain, or within three miles of the shore thereof, dies of or is slaughtered in consequence of being affected with a contagious or infectious disease, the master of the vessel shall, with all practicable speed, cause the carcass thereof to be disinfected on board the vessel in such mode as the privy council from time to time may direct or approve.

If he fails to do so, he shall be deemed guilty of an offense against this order.

6. If any person throws or places, or causes or suffers to be thrown or placed, into or in any river, stream, canal, or other water in Great Britain, or into or in the sea within three miles of the shore of Great Britain, the carcass of an animal (including a horse) which has died of or been slaughtered in consequence of being affected with a contagious or infectious disease, he shall be deemed guilty of an offense against this order, unless he shows to the satisfaction of the justices before whom he is charged that he

did not know that the same had so died or been slaughtered, and that he could not with reasonable diligence have obtained that knowledge.

7. It shall not be lawful for any person, except with the license of the privy council, to dig up, or cause to be dug up, the carcass or any part of the carcass of any animal (including a horse) buried under a regulation of a local authority or under the direction of a receiver of wreck.

If any person acts in contravention of this article he shall be deemed guilty of an offense against this order.

PART V.—SLAUGHTER IN CATTLE-PLAGUE; COMPENSATION.

65. Every local authority shall cause all animals affected with cattle-plague within their district to be slaughtered.

66. A local authority may, if they think fit, cause to be slaughtered any animal that has been in the same shed or stable, or in the same herd or flock, or in contact with any animal affected with cattle-plague within their district.

67. Where an animal is affected with disease suspected to be cattle-plague the local authority may cause the animal to be slaughtered in order to ascertain the nature of the disease.

68. Where an animal affected with cattle-plague, or affected with disease suspected to be cattle-plague, is slaughtered in pursuance of this act, the local authority (except as otherwise provided in this act) shall, by way of compensation for the animal, pay to the owner thereof such sum, not exceeding twenty pounds and not exceeding one-half of the value of the animal immediately before it was affected with cattle-plague, as to the local authority seems fit.

69. When a local authority causes an animal to be slaughtered on account of it having been in the same shed or stable, or in the same herd or flock, or in contact with an animal affected with cattle-plague, the owner of the animal so slaughtered may either dispose of the carcass on his own account, with a license from some officer appointed in that behalf by the local authority, or may require the local authority to dispose of the same, in which latter case the local authority shall pay to the owner thereof, by way of compensation, such sum, not exceeding thirty pounds, as may equal three-fourths of the value of the animal slaughtered.

70. A local authority may require the value of any animal slaughtered under this act to be ascertained by officers of the local authority or by arbitration, and generally may impose conditions as to evidence of the slaughter and value of the animals slaughtered.

71. A local authority may, if they think fit, withhold compensation in respect to any animal slaughtered, where the owner or the person having the charge thereof has in their judgment been guilty, in relation to such animal, of any act in contravention of this act, or of any order, regulation, or license of the privy council or a local authority, or has, in relation to such animal, failed to comply with the provisions of this act, or of any such order, regulation, or license in respect of the giving of notice of disease or in any other respect, and may, if they think fit, withhold compensation in respect of a foreign animal slaughtered on account of it being affected with cattle-plague, or with disease suspected to be cattle-plague, if it appears to them that the animal was so affected at the time of the landing thereof.

72. Where an animal has been slaughtered in pursuance of this act the owner thereof shall not be entitled to recover in respect of the insurance thereof any sum which, together with the payment which he receives for the same under this act, would exceed the sum which he would have been entitled to receive in respect of the insurance.

73. The privy council may, notwithstanding anything in this act, reserve for experimental treatment any animal ordered to be slaughtered under this act, but compensation shall be payable in respect thereof as if this section had not been enacted.

74. Every local authority shall keep, in such manner and form as the privy council from time to time by order direct or approve, a record relative to proceedings under this part of this act, stating the date of any order for slaughter, and the execution of the order, or the reservation of the animal for experimental treatment (as the case may be), and other proper particulars, and such record shall be evidence if any question arises concerning an order for the slaughter of any animal, or concerning compensation in respect thereof.

PART VI.—ORDERS OF COUNCIL AND LOCAL AUTHORITIES.

75. The privy council may from time to time make such orders as they think expedient for all or any of the following purposes:

For insuring for animals brought by sea to ports in Great Britain a proper supply of food and water during the passage and on landing.

For protecting such animals from unnecessary suffering during the passage and on landing.

For protecting animals from unnecessary suffering during inland transit.

For prohibiting or regulating the movement of animals, and the removal of dead animals or parts thereof, and of hay, straw, litter, dung, and other things likely to spread contagious or infectious diseases among animals.

For requiring the cleansing and disinfecting of yards, sheds, stables, fields, and other premises.

For regulating the disposal of animals dying while affected with a contagious or infectious disease.

For requiring notice of the appearance of any such disease among animals.

For prohibiting or regulating the holding markets, fairs, exhibitions or sales of animals.

And generally any orders whatsoever, which they think it expedient to make for the better execution of this act, or for the purpose of in any manner preventing the introduction or spreading of contagious or infectious disease among animals in Great Britain (whether any such orders are of the same kind as the kinds enumerated in this section or not), and may in any such order direct or authorize the slaughtering of animals that are affected with any contagious or infectious disease, or that have been in contact with animals so affected; and may in any such order direct or authorize the local authority to pay compensation for any animals so slaughtered; and may in any such order impose penalties for offenses against the same, not exceeding the sum of twenty pounds for any such offense, and so that in every such order provision he made that a penalty less than the maximum may be ordered to be paid; and this section shall extend to horses and all ruminating animals not within the definition of animals in this act.

Every such order shall have the like force and effect as if it had been enacted by this act.

76. A person, for the time being, appointed by the privy council an inspector for the purposes of this act shall have for and throughout Great Britain all such powers, authorities. and privileges as an inspector of a local authority has within or in relation to his district; and a direction of the privy council shall in the case of an inspector appointed by them to be deemed equivalent to a direction of a local authority in the case of an inspector appointed by them.

77. The privy council may from time to time, by order, declare that such of the provisions of this act, and of any order of the privy council under it, as relates to the metropolis, or any of these provisions, shall also extend and apply to any town, city, parish, or place specified in the order, and the same shall extend to such town, city, parish, or place accordingly; and the privy council may at any time revoke or from time to time vary any such order.

78. The privy council may from time to time, by order, make such regulations as they think expedient for prohibiting or regulating the landing of any hay, straw, fodder, or other article brought from any place out of the United Kingdom, whereby it appears to the privy council contagion or infection may be conveyed to animals, or for causing the same to be destroyed if landed.

If any person lands, or attempts to land, any hay, straw, fodder, or other article in contravention of any such order the same shall be forfeited in like manner as goods the importation whereof is prohibited by the acts relating to the customs are liable to be forfeited; and the person so offending shall be liable to such penalties as are imposed on persons importing or attempting to import goods the importation whereof is prohibited by the acts relating to the customs, without prejudice to any proceeding against him under this act or any such order, but so that no person be punished twice for the same offense.

79. The privy council may require a local authority to carry into effect any order of the privy council under this act, and may authorize a local authority to make any regulations for the purpose of preventing the spreading of contagious or infectious diseases among animals, subject to such conditions as the privy council impose; and the local authority may by any such regulation impose such penalties as the privy council are by this act authorized to impose by order.

80. The expenses incurred by a local authority in executing any order of the privy council under this act shall be defrayed by the local authority out of such local rates or funds as such order directs, and the subject to or in the absence of any such direction shall be deemed expenses incurred by the local authority in pursuance of this act.

81. Every order of the privy council under this act shall be published in the London Gazette, save that where an order of the privy council affects only a particular port, town, or place, or part thereof, specified in the order, or declares a place to be an infected place, or to be free from cattle-plague or from sheep-pox, or is in the nature of a license under an order of council, or of a revocation of such a license, then the insertion in the London Gazette of a notice of the issuing thereof shall be for all purposes sufficient publication thereof.

Any order of the privy council under this act shall be published by and at the expense of any local authority to whom the same is sent by the privy council for publication, in some newspaper circulating in the district of the local authority, or in such other manner as the privy council direct.

Any order or regulation made by a local authority shall be published by them, at their own expense, in such manner as the privy council direct and subject to, or, in the absence of any such direction, in such manner as the local authority think sufficient and proper to insure publicity.

82. Any order, license, regulation, or other instrument made under this act or under any order of the privy council thereunder, may be in writing or print, or partly in writing and partly in print.

83. No stamp duty shall be payable on, and no fee or other charge shall be demanded or made for, any appointment, certificate, declaration, or license under this act, or any order or regulation made thereunder.

84. An order or regulation made or issued by a local authority under this act or under any order of the privy council may be proved as follows:

By the production of a copy of a newspaper containing a copy of such order or regulation; or

By the production of a printed copy of such order or regulation purporting to be certified to be a true copy by the clerk of the peace where the authority are justices in general or quarter sessions assembled, or by the town clerk or other officer performing the duties of a town clerk in the case of an authority having a town clerk or other officer as aforesaid, or by such other officer as the privy council prescribes.

And any such order or regulation shall, until the contrary is proved, be deemed to have been duly made and issued at the time at which it bears date.

85. Penalties and forfeitures shall be recoverable and applicable under an order of the privy council or an order or regulation of a local authority, as penalties and forfeitures under this act are recoverable and applicable.

PART VII.—LANDS.

86. A local authority may purchase or take on lease or at a rent land for the purpose of burying therein animals dying of or slaughtered on account of any contagious or infectious disease, or for the purpose of providing wharves, lairs, sheds, markets, houses, and places for the landing, reception, sale, and slaughter of foreign animals, or for any other purpose of this act, and may sell, exchange, or dispose of lands acquired by them under this act, but not required to be retained for the purposes thereof, carrying the money produced thereby to the credit of the local rate.

87. Land purchased or taken on lease or at a rent under this act by a local authority, not being a body corporate, shall be assured or demised to the local authority and their successors, in trust for the purposes of this act, and shall be accepted, taken, and held by them as a body corporate.

88. The regulations contained in section seventy-five of the local government act, 1858, shall be observed with respect to the purchase of land by a local authority for the purposes of this act, and shall apply and have effect as if the local authority were a local board acting under the local government act, and the purposes of this act were purposes of that act, save that the advertisements and notices requisite under that section may be published and served in any two consecutive months instead of only in the months therein specified, and that the local rate be substituted for the rates therein mentioned; and the powers conferred by this section may be exercised by a local authority with respect to land either within and without their district.

PART VIII.—EXPENSES OF LOCAL AUTHORITIES.

89. The expenditure of a local authority in compensation for animals slaughtered under Part V of this act, or in respect of principal of or interest on money borrowed in pursuance of this act, shall be defrayed out of the local rate, or out of a separate rate to be levied in all respects as the local rate, and included under the term local rate.

Any person who is not the owner of the premises in respect of which he is rated under this section to the local rate may deduct from the growing rent due to the owner of such premises one-half of the rate payable by him for the purposes of this section, and every owner shall allow such deduction accordingly.

The owner for the purposes of this section shall be the person for the time being entitled to receive the rack rent of the premises in respect of which the rate is made on his own account, or who would be entitled to receive the same if such premises were let at a rack-rent, including under the term rack-rent any rent which is not less than two-thirds of the net annual value of the premises out of which the rent issues.

Every local authority shall have power, notwithstanding any limit in any act of Parliament, to levy a local rate to the amount required for the purposes of this act, but every rate or increase of rate levied under this section shall in all precepts for the levy thereof be described as a separate rate or separate item of rate, and when collected from the individual rate-payers shall be collected as a separate rate or specified as a separate item of rate.

Every order of a board of guardians for contributions of monies, out of which any such expenditure as in this section mentioned is payable, shall state the amount, in the pound of contribution, required for such expenditure; and the overseers, on the receipt given to any rate-payer for poor rate, shall specify the amount (if any) collected in respect of such expenditure.

90. Expenses incurred by a local authority in pursuance of this act, other than in their expenditure in compensation for animals slaughtered under Part V of this act, or in respect of principal of or interest on money borrowed in pursuance of this act, shall be defrayed out of the local rate.

91. Where before the twentieth day of February, one thousand eight hundred and sixty-six, any person suffered so great a loss of cattle by cattle-plague as to entitle him, after the passing of this act, in the opinion of the local authority, to a remission in whole or in part of the amount due from him in respect of the local rate, such remission may be granted by the local authority.

92. Where, at the passing of this act, a local authority have in their hands an unappropriated balance of a local rate levied under any act repealed by this act, they may if they think fit, apply any part of such balance in compensation for cattle slaughtered between the passing of "the cattle-disease prevention act, 1866," and the appointment of inspectors under that act, by direction of a person whom the owner of such cattle had reasonable ground to believe to be the authorized inspector for the execution of the act, or they may carry such balance, or any part thereof, to the credit of the ordinary account of the local rate, to be applied for any of the purposes for which the local rate, when levied under any act other than an act repealed by this act, is applicable.

93. All precepts, orders for contribution, and forms of poor rate shall, where necessary, be varied in such manner as may be required for carrying into effect this act.

94. The treasurer of a local authority may, if directed by them, advance out of any monies for the time being in his hands, any sum required for payment of expenses incurred by them in pursuance of this act.

95. Where the local rate is a county rate or borough rate, or any other such rate as is mentioned in the second schedule to this act, all the provisions of the statutes applicable to the making, levying, and collecting of a county rate, borough rate, or such other rate shall apply, notwithstanding that the whole of such rate, or any part thereof, is applicable to the payment of the expenditure of a local authority in pursuance of this act, in compensation for animals slaughtered, or in respect of principal of or interest on money borrowed in pursuance of this act.

96. An error in the statement of the amount of expenses in any precept, warrant, contribution, order, or receipt issued or given under this act shall not invalidate such precept, warrant, contribution, order, or receipt; but any person aggrieved by the error may appeal to the justices in petty sessions and the justices may rectify the error and award to the appellant compensation for any loss he may have sustained thereby, the amount of such compensation to be paid to the appellant, and to be deemed expenses of the local authority under this act.

97. Notwithstanding anything in this act, the local authority of each borough situate within a county and assessed to the county rate thereof, shall be recouped the proportionate amount contributed by the borough to the expenses incurred by the local authority of the county in pursuance of this act, including expenditure in compensation for animals slaughtered, or in respect of principal of or interest on money borrowed in pursuance of this act, so that the burden of those expenses shall be borne wholly by the county, and not as to any part thereof, by any borough situate within the county.

Borrowing.

98. Where the rate levied or required for the purposes of this act exceeds or would exceed sixpence in the pound, a local authority may, for the purposes of defraying any costs, charges, and expenses under this act, borrow at interest on the credit of the local rate any sums of money necessary for defraying such costs, charges, and expenses; and for the purpose of securing the repayment of any sums of money so borrowed, together with such interest as aforesaid, the local authority may mortgage the local rate for any period not exceeding seven years.

Where the rate levied or required for the purposes of this act exceeds or would exceed ninepence in the pound, the commissioners of Her Majesty's treasury may, on application from the local authority, extend the term to any term not exceeding fourteen years, and the local authority may mortgage the rate accordingly: Provided that where the local authority borrow for any purpose of this act on any security other than the local rate (whether together with the local rate, if any, or separately therefrom), the limitations in this section contained respecting the amount of rate and the term of years shall not operate.

The provisions of the commissioners' clauses act, 1847, with respect to the mortgages to be executed by the commissioners shall be incorporated with this section, the local authority being deemed to be the commissioners, and any mortgagee or assignee may enforce payment of his principal and interest by appointment of a receiver.

The public-works loan commissioners may, with the approval of the commissioners of Her Majesty's treasury, advance to a local authority, on the security, of the local rate, without any further security, any sums of money to be applied for the purposes of this act, and to be repaid with interest within any period as aforesaid.

99. Where the estimated amount of the sum required to be levied for payment of the expenditure of a local authority in pursuance of this act (including expenditure incurred in the payment of money borrowed or of interest thereon) exceeds the sum that would be raised by the levying of a rate of one shilling in the pound on the ratable value of the property assessed to the local rate, the local authority may borrow from the public-works loan commissioners, and the public-works loan commissioners may, out of the balance for the time being unapplied of any money by any act already passed authorized to be issued for the purposes of loans under any act repealed by this act, or out of any other money for the time being authorized to be issued for the purpose of loans under this section, lend to them such sums as may be required, subject to the following conditions:

(1.) Every such loan shall be made with the sanction of the commissioners of Her Majesty's treasury.

(2.) Interest shall be at the rate of 3¼ per centum per annum.

(3.) Repayment of the loan shall be made by such number of equal annual installments, not exceeding thirty, as the commissioners of Her Majesty's treasury direct.

(4.) The commissioners of Her Majesty's treasury may, if they think fit, authorize the postponement, for a period not exceeding two years, of any payment of principal or interest becoming due within the first three years.

(5.) Repayment of the loan and interest shall be secured by a mortgage of the local rate, and it shall not be incumbent on the public works loan commissioners to require any other security.

(6) The local authority shall have power to levy, and shall levy, rates requisite for the purpose of repaying the loan with interest.

(7.) The sanction of the commissioners of Her Majesty's treasury to the loan shall be conclusive evidence that it is authorized by this act; and no objection shall be made by any rate-payer to the validity of any mortgage for the loan, or to the application of the proceeds of the local rate to the payment of the principal or interest of the loan.

(8.) The commissioners of Her Majesty's treasury may, by agreement with the local authority borrowing, commute into one equivalent annuity, terminable at the time fixed for the liquidation of the annual installments aforesaid, the payments secured by the mortgage, or any portion of such payments.

100. Where a local authority have borrowed money on the security of a mortgage of the local rate, under any act repealed by this act, then (except as otherwise provided in this act with respect to the county of Chester) notwithstanding any repeal in this act, or any alteration made by this act in the definition of a local authority or local rate, or any other thing in this act contained, the local rate mortgaged shall continue to be the security for the money borrowed, as if this act had not been passed; and in relation to the money so borrowed the local authority which borrowed such money, and the local rate on which the same is charged, shall continue to be the local authority and the local rate under the acts repealed by this act as if this act had not been passed ; and all provisions of Part II of the cattle-diseases prevention act, 1866, relative to expenses, and all the provisions of the cattle-diseases prevention amendment act, 1866, and all other provisions of any act repealed by this act relative to expenses, and all the provisions of the cattle-diseases prevention amendment act, 1866, and all other provisions of any act repealed by this act relative to expenses of local authorities, rating, remission of rates, and borrowing, and matters connected therewith respectively, shall, in relation to the money so borrowed, and to the rate charged therewith, continue to operate as if this act had not been passed.

101. With respect to the county of Chester the following provisions shall have effect :

(1.) As far as regards the expenditure of the local authority of the county of Chester in respect of principal of or interest on money borrowed in pursuance of any act repealed by this act, and any matter consequent on or relative to that expenditure (including the remission of rates), the foregoing provisions of this part of this act shall not apply to that county.

(2.) That expenditure shall be defrayed out of the county rate for the county of Chester, or out of any money applicable under any act of Parliament, or otherwise, for the public charges or uses of that county, or partly out of one and partly of the other;

s ich county rate to be assessed, levied, and collected in the manner prescribed by law for the assessment, levying, and collection of county rates, independently of this act or of any act repealed by this act.

(3.) In lieu of any provision authorizing deduction by tenant from landlord of half of the local rate, any person who is not the owner of the premises in the county of Chester in respect of which he is rated to the poor rate may, in each year until the first day of November, one thousand eight hundred and ninety-six, in which he duly pays his poor rate, deduct from the growing rent due to the owner of such premises a sum equal to one penny in the pound on the annual ratable value of such premises, and every owner shall allow such deduction accordingly; and the owner, for the purposes of this section, shall be the person defined as such in this part of this act.

(4.) The local authority for the county of Chester shall entertain and decide on applications from rate-payers to whom, if this section had not been inserted in this act, remission in respect of the local rate might have been granted, and may, on such applications, grant to the applicants, or any of them, such sum or sums of money (if any) out of the county rate as the local authority think reasonable, regard being had to the extent of loss in the cases of the several applicants.

(5.) The local authority of each borough situate within the county of Chester and assessed to the county rate thereof, shall, by means of repayment out of the county rate, or by means of differential rates, or partly in the one way and partly in the other, be recouped the proportionate amount contributed by the borough to any money granted as aforesaid, so that the burden of the expenditure incurred by the local authority of the county in respect of such grants shall be borne wholly by the county, and not as to any part thereof by any borough situate within the county; but nothing in this section shall prejudicially affect the mortgage security of the public-works loan commissioners for money advanced to the local authority of the county of Chester under any act repealed by this act; and the local authority of that county shall, from time to time, levy such rates as are under this section applicable, and as are for the time being requisite (either wholly or in conjunction with such other money as in this section mentioned) for the purpose of repaying with interest the money advanced on such mortgage security according to the terms thereof.

102. The existence of any order or precept for the making or collection under any act repealed by this act of any rate remaining uncollected, wholly or in part, at the passing of this act shall not affect the validity of any rate made after the passing of this act.

PART IX.—OFFENSES AND LEGAL PROCEEDINGS.

103. If any person acts in contravention of or is guilty of any offense against this act, or any order or regulation made by the privy council or a local authority in pursuance of this act, he shall for every such offense (except as otherwise provided in this act, and except where a less penalty is provided in any such order or regulation) be liable to a penalty not exceeding twenty pounds.

Where any such offense is committed with respect to more than four animals a penalty not exceeding five pounds for each animal may be imposed instead of the penalty of twenty pounds.

Where any such offense is committed in relation to offal, dung, hay, straw, litter, or anything, a further penalty, not exceeding ten pounds, may be imposed in respect of every half ton in weight of such offal, or other thing, after the first half ton.

104. If any person does any of the following things he shall be deemed guilty of an offense against this act :

(1.) If he does anything for which a license is requisite under this act, or any order of the privy council thereunder, without having obtained a license.

(2.) If where such a license is requisite, having obtained a license in that behalf, he does the thing licensed after the license has expired.

(3.) If he uses or offers or attempts to use as such a license an instrument not being a complete license, or an instrument untruly purporting or appearing to be a license, unless he shows to the satisfaction of the justices before whom he is charged that he did not know of such incompleteness or untruth, and that he could not with reasonable diligence have obtained such knowledge.

(4.) If with intent to evade any provision of this act, or of any order of the privy council thereunder, he fabricates or alters, or offers or utters, knowing the same to be fabricated or altered, any license, declaration, certificate, or instrument made or issued, or purporting to be made or issued, under or for any purpose of this act or any such order.

(5.) If for the purpose of obtaining any license, certificate, or instrument under or for the purposes of any such provision, he makes a declaration false in any material particular, unless he shows to the satisfaction of the justices before whom he is charged that he did not know of such falsity, and that he could not with reasonable diligence have obtained such knowledge.

(6.) If he obtains or endeavors to obtain any such license, certificate, or instrument, by means of any false pretense, unless he shows to the satisfaction of the justices before whom he is charged that he did not know of such falsity, and he could not with reasonable diligence have obtained such knowledge.

(7.) If he grants or issues any such license, certificate, or instrument, being false in any material particular, unless he shows to the satisfaction of the justices before whom he is charged that he did not know of such falsity, and that he could not with reasonable diligence have obtained such knowledge.

And in any such case he shall be liable, on conviction, in discretion of the justices, to be imprisoned for any term not exceeding three months, with or without hard labor, in lieu of the pecuniary penalty to which he is liable under this act.

105. If any person obstructs or impedes an inspector or other officer acting in execution of this act, or of any order of the privy council thereunder, he, and every person aiding and assisting him therein, shall be guilty of an offense against this act, and the inspector or other officer, or any person whom he calls to his assistance, may seize the offender and detain him until he can be conveniently taken before a justice, to be dealt with according to law.

106. Notwithstanding anything in any act relating to the metropolitan police or to municipal corporations, or in any other act, one-half of every penalty or forfeiture recovered under this act shall be paid to the person who sues or proceeds for the same, and the other half shall be applied as if this section had not been enacted.

107. In proceedings before justices under this act any railway company or other body corporate may appear by any member of their board of directors or council, or by any officer authorized in writing under the hand of any director or member of the council of the company or body.

108. If any party feels aggrieved by the dismissal of his complaint by justices, or by any determination or adjudication of justices with respect to any penalty or forfeiture under this act, he may appeal therefrom, subject to the conditions and regulations following :

(1.) The appeal shall be made to some court of general or quarter sessions for the county or place in which the cause of appeal has arisen, holden not less than fifteen days and not more than four months after the decision of the justices.

(2.) The appellant shall, within three days after the cause of appeal has arisen, give notice to the clerk of the petty sessional division for which the justices act whose decision is appealed from, of his intention to appeal and of the grounds thereof.

(3.) The appellant shall immediately after such notice enter into a recognizance, before a justice of the peace, with two sufficient sureties, conditioned personally to try such appeal, and to abide the judgment of the court thereon, and to pay such costs as may be awarded by the court.

(4.) The court may adjourn the appeal and may make such order thereon as they think just. But nothing in this section respecting appeals shall affect any enactment relative to appeals in cases of summary convictions or adjudications in the city of London or the metropolitan police district.

109. For the purposes of proceedings under this act, or any order of the privy council or order or regulation of a local authority thereunder, every offense against this act or any such order or regulation shall be deemed to have arisen, either in the place in which the same actually was committed or arose, or in any place in which the person charged or complained against happens to be.

Protection of persons in execution of act.

110. An action or proceeding shall not lie against any person acting or intending to act under the authority or in the execution or in pursuance of this act for any alleged irregularity or trespass or other act or thing done or omitted by him under this act, unless notice in writing (specifying the cause of the action or proceeding, and the name and residence of the intending plaintiff or prosecutor, and of his attorney or agent in the matter) is given by the intending plaintiff or prosecutor to the intended defendant one month at least before the commencement of the action or proceeding, nor unless the action or proceeding is commenced within four months next after the doing of such damage has ceased; and any such action shall be laid and tried in the county or place where the cause of action arose, and not elsewhere.

111. In any such action the defendant may plead generally that the act or thing complained of was done or omitted by him when acting or intending to act under the authority or in the execution or in pursuance of this act, and may give all special matter in evidence.

112. On the trial of any such action the plaintiff shall not be permitted to go into evidence of any cause of action not stated in his notice.

113. The plaintiff in any such action shall not succeed if tender of sufficient amends is made by the defendant before the commencement of the action ; and in case no tender has been made the defendant may, by leave of the court in which the action is brought, at any time pay into the court such sum of money as he thinks fit, where-

upon such proceeding and order shall be had and made in and by the court as may be had and made on the payment of money into court in an ordinary action.

114. If in any such action the plaintiff does not succeed in obtaining judgment, the defendant shall receive such full and reasonable indemnity as to all costs, charges, and expenses incurred in and about the action as may be taxed and allowed by the proper officer, subject to review ; and though a verdict is given for the plaintiff in the action, he shall not have costs against the defendant unless the judge before whom the trial is had certifies his approval of the action and verdict.

115. Where any such action or proceeding is defended under the direction or with the approval of the local authority, the costs, charges, and expenses incurred in and about the same, by or on behalf of the defendant and payable by him, and any damage or other money recovered against or payable by him in or in consequence of such action or proceeding, shall be deemed expenses incurred by the local authority in pursuance of this act and shall be defrayed accordingly.

Part X.—Scotland.

116. The provisions of this part of this act shall extend to Scotland only, and shall have effect in substitution for the provisions of the preceding parts of this act, when so expressed or implied, and otherwise shall have effect in addition to the provisions thereof.

117. For the purposes of this act the respective districts, authorities, rate, and officers described in that behalf in the ninth schedule to this act shall be the district, the local authority, the local rate, and the clerk of the local authority.

118. The commissioners of supply in every county shall meet and nominate not fewer than four or more than fifteen of their number to act on the county board for the purposes of this act, and shall intimate to the lord lieutenant of the county and the convener of the county the number and names of the persons so appointed.

The clerk of supply in each county shall call a meeting of the occupiers of agricultural subjects in such county, valued in the valuation roll in force for the time at one hundred pounds and upwards, and of occupiers of such subjects of which they are owners valued in the valuation roll at fifty pounds and under one hundred pounds; and such meeting shall be called by advertisement in one or more newspapers circulating in the county for the same day as, or for a day not later than eight days after the meeting of the commissioners of supply, and such advertisement shall specify the time and place of such meeting, and the clerk of supply shall be clerk to such meeting; and the meeting shall nominate from among such occupiers, and owners and occupiers, a number of persons equal to those nominated by the commissioners of supply; and the meeting shall also name a convener, who shall intimate the names of the persons so nominated to the convener of the county, and shall have power to call similar meetings by such advertisement, when occasion shall require ; and in the event of such election not being intimated to the convener of the county within fifteen days from the date of such meeting, it shall be lawful to the lord lieutenant to nominate from among such occupiers, or owners and occupiers, such number of persons, and intimate the same to the convener of the county.

Any such nomination and intimation made for the purposes of any act repealed by this act shall continue to have effect for the purposes of this act.

Vacancies from time to time happening by death, resignation, or otherwise among the members of the local authority shall be filled up by the authority and in the manner by and in which the members vacating office were respectively nominated.

The persons nominated as in this section provided, and the lord lieutenant of the county, the convener of the county, and the sheriff of the county (or in his absence such one of his substitutes within the county as he directs by writing under his hand) for the time being, shall constitute the local authority ; five shall be a quorum of the local authority.

As far as not otherwise provided by this act, such local authority shall have all the powers conferred on the local authority by this act, and shall have power to elect a chairman, specify a quorum, and make all regulations necessary for carrying the purposes of this act into effect.

The chairman of the local authority, and in default of him the convener of the county, and in default of him any three members of the local authority, may at any time call a meeting of the local authority, to be held at such time and place as he or they may fix, and the local authority may adjourn as they from time to time think fit.

119. Part VII of this act shall have effect as if section ninety of the public health . (Scotland) act, 1867, were thereby applied, instead of section seventy-five of the local government act, 1858; and in the said section ninety the local authority and local rate under this act shall be substituted for the local authority and the assessment therein mentioned.

120. The local authority in a county shall from time to time give notice to the commissioners of supply of the sums necessary to be provided under the provisions of this

act by means of the local rate; and the amount so intimated shall be assessed and collected by the commissioners of supply according to the real rent of lands and heritages as appearing on the valuation roll in force for the year, who shall pay over the same to the local authority.

The local authority in a burgh shall in like manner assess and collect the amount required to be raised by local rate within such burgh.

All such assessments shall be payable one-half by the proprietor and one-half by the tenant, but may be collected wholly from the tenant, who shall in that case be entitled to deduct one-half thereof from the rent payable by him to the proprietor, who shall in that case be entitled to relief against the tenant for one-half of the assessment; and for the purposes of the provisions of this act relative to any balance of funds remaining over from any assessment, the words "local rate" shall in Scotland mean the poor rate.

All the provisions in regard to the recovery of assessments in the act of the session of the twentieth and twenty-first years of Her Majesty (chapter 72), "to render more effectual the police in counties and burghs in Scotland," are hereby incorporated in this act, as far as the same are not inconsistent with the provisions of this act.

121. In the case of a county, a printed copy of an order or regulation of the local authority, purporting to be certified to be a true copy by the clerk of supply, shall be received in proof.

122. The terms "justice" and "justices" shall include any magistrate having jurisdiction under the summary-procedure act, 1864.

123. In the event of any person refusing or delaying to comply with the order of a local authority, the local authority may give information thereof to the procurator-fiscal of the county or burgh, who may apply to the sheriff for a warrant to carry such order into effect, and such warrant may be executed by the officers of the court in the usual way.

124. All judicial powers given to justices and quarter-sessions, or to magistrates in boroughs, by this act, may also be exercised by the sheriff of the county or the sheriff substitute.

125. Notice of appeal and of the grounds thereof shall be given to the clerk of the peace of the county.

126. For the purposes of this act the burgh of Maxwelltown shall be held to be a part of the stewartry of Kirkcudbright, and not of the parliamentary burgh of Dumfries.

SCHEDULES.

The first schedule relates to acts repealed.

The second schedule refers to the local authorities, &c., in England.

District of local authority.	Description of local authority of district set opposite name.	Local rate.	Clerk of local authority.
Counties except the metropolis.	The justices in general or quarter sessions assembled.	The county rate, or rate in the nature of a county rate.	Clerk of the peace.
The metropolis (subject to the provisions of this act respecting the city of London and the liberties thereof.)	The metropolitan board of works.	Rate or fund applicable to the payment of the general expenses of the board.	The clerk of the metropolitan board of works.
Boroughs	The mayor, aldermen, and burgesses acting by the council.	The borough fund or borough rate.	Town clerk.
	Where the borough is not subject to the act of the session of the fifth and sixth years of the reign of King William the Fourth, chapter seventy-six, the commissioners or other body maintaining the police therein.	The rate applicable by the commissioners or other body to the maintenance of the police.	Clerk of the commissioners or other body.
District of local board of Oxford.	The local board............	Rate leviable by the local rate.	Clerk of the local board.

The third schedule contains regulations respecting committees and subcommittees:

" 1. A committee formed by a local authority may consist wholly of members of the local authority, or partly thereof, and partly of such other persons being rated occupiers in the district and qualified in such other manner as the local authority determine.

" 2. A committee of a local authority and a subcommittee of an executive committee may elect a chairman of their meetings.

" 3. If no chairman is elected, or if the chairman elected is not present at the time appointed for the holding of a meeting, the members then present shall choose one of their number to be chairman of the meeting.

" 4. A committee or subcommittee may meet and adjourn as they think proper.

" 5. Every question at a meeting of a committee or subcommittee shall be determined by a majority of votes of the members present and voting on the question, and in case of an equal division of votes the chairman shall have a second or casting vote."

The fourth schedule refers to regulations that may be applied to the landing, movement, and disposal of foreign animals:

" 1. These regulations are to have effect with respect to those foreign animals to which they are from time to time applied by order of the privy council.

" 2. Those foreign animals are to be landed only at parts of ports defined by special orders of the privy council for the several ports as places where foreign animals may be landed.

" 3. They are to be landed in such manner, within such times, and subject to such supervision and control as the commissioners of customs from time to time direct.

" 4. The owner, consignee, or other person landing them is either before landing them or within twelve hours after landing them, at his own expense, to mark them as follows : In case of cattle, by clipping the hair off the end of the tail, and in such further manner (if any) as the privy council from time to time prescribe, and in case of other animals in such manner as the privy council from time to time prescribe.

" They are not to be moved from the place of landing or lairs adjacent thereto, approved by the privy council, except as follows:

"(a.) After the expiration of twelve hours from the time of landing or such other period as the privy council from time to time prescribe.

"(b.) On a certificate from the veterinary inspector appointed in this behalf by the commissioners of customs, certifying that they are free from contagious or infectious disease.

" 6. They are not to be moved alive out of the part of the port of landing from time to time defined in that behalf by the privy council.

" 7. Notwithstanding anything in these regulations, where a vessel comes into port having on board foreign animals maimed or injured on the voyage, the owner, consignee, or other person in charge thereof, or the master of the vessel, shall, if directed by the veterinary inspector aforesaid, or may, if he thinks fit, slaughter those animals any of them immediately on their being landed, but the carcass, hide, skin, hair, wool, horn, hoof, or offal of any such animal or any part thereof is not to be moved from the place of landing, or some lair or slaughter house adjacent thereto approved by the privy council, without a certificate from the veterinary inspector aforesaid, certifying that it is not likely to introduce or spread contagious or infectious disease."

The fifth schedule has reference to the tolls and dues levied in the metropolitan market after opening of foreign cattle market.

Sheep, per head...Five farthings.
Beasts, per head..Sixpence.
Calves, per head...Threepence.
Pigs, per head...Five farthings.

The sixth schedule contains " Rules with respect to infected places."

PART I.—CATTLE PLAGUE.

1. The rules of this part of this schedule are to have effect with respect to infected places as regards cattle plague.

2. No animal is to be moved alive out of an infected place.

3. Any hide, skin, hair, wool, horn, hoof, or offal of any animal, or any part thereof, is not to be moved out of an infected place without a license signed by an officer of the local authority appointed to issue licenses in that behalf, certifying either that the thing moved has not formed part of an animal affected with cattle plague; or if an animal that has been in the same shed or stable, or in the same herd or flock, or in contact with an animal so affected, or that the thing moved has been disinfected.

4. The carcass of an animal, or a single portion of raw meat weighing more than twenty pounds, is not to be moved out of an infected place without a license signed by an officer of the local authority appointed in that behalf certifying that the car-

cass or meat moved is not the carcass or part of the carcass of an animal affected with the cattle plague.

5. Any dung of animals, and any hay, straw, litter, or other thing commonly used for food of animals, or otherwise for or about animals, is not to be moved out of an infected place without a license signed by an officer of the locality appointed in that behalf, certifying that the thing moved has not been in contact with or been used for or about any animal affected with cattle plague, or that it has been disinfected.

PART II.—SHEEP-POX.

1. The rules of this part of this schedule are to have effect with respect to infected places as regards sheep-pox.

2. No sheep is to be moved alive out of an infected place.

3. Any skin, wool, horn, or hoof of any sheep, or any part thereof, is not to be moved out of an infected place without a license signed by an officer appointed by the local authority to issue licenses in that behalf, certifying that the thing moved did not belong to any sheep forming part of a flock affected with sheep-pox, or to any sheep that has been on a place in which that disease existed.

4. Sheds and places used by sheep affected with sheep-pox are forthwith, after being so used, to be cleansed and disinfected.

The seventh schedule contains "pleuro-pneumonia rules."

1. These rules are to have effect with respect to any field, stable, cow-shed, or other premises infected by pleuro-pneumonia.

2. Cattle affected by pleuro-pneumonia are not to be moved from such field, stable, cow-shed, or other premises or from any land or building contiguous thereto, in the same occupation, except for immediate slaughter, and according to regulations to be from time to time made by the local authority for insuring such slaughter.

3. Other cattle are not to be moved from such field, stable, cow-shed, or other premises, or from any land or building contiguous thereto in the same occupation, except for immediate slaughter, without a license signed by an officer of the local authority appointed to issue licenses in that behalf, certifying that the cattle moved are not affected with pleuro-pneumonia, and have not been in the same shed or herd or in contact with cattle so affected.

4. Sheds and places used by cattle affected with pleuro-pneumonia are forthwith after being so used to be cleansed and disinfected to the satisfaction of the local authority.

The eighth schedule gives the forms to be used by the inspector.

(1.)

Declaration of diseases.

[The contagious diseases (animals) act, 1869.]

I, A. B., of ——— , the inspector appointed by ——— , being the local authority for the county of ——— , hereby declare that I have this day found cattle plague [or pleuro-pneumonia or sheep-pox] to exist in the following field, stable, cow-shed, or other premises (that is to say) [here describe the place where the disease is found].

Dated this —— day of ———, 18—— .

(Signed)

A. B.

(2.)

Notice of declaration to occupiers.

[The contagious diseases (animals) act, 1869.]

To C. D., of ——— :

I, A. B., of ———, inspector appointed by ———, being the local authority for the [county] of ———, hereby give you notice, as the occupier of the following field, stable, cow-shed, or other premises (that is to say), [here describe the place where the disease is found], that I have made a declaration, a copy whereof is indorsed on this notice [copy of declaration as filled up and signed to be indorsed], and that in consequence thereof *the field, stable, cow-shed, or other premises aforesaid, with all lands and buildings contiguous thereto in your occupation, have become and are an infected place, and that the same will continue to be an infected place* until the determination and declaration relative thereto of the local authority, as provided for in section of —— of the above-mentioned act [or in case of pleuro-pneumonia omit the part between the asterisks, and insert the pleuro-pneumonia rules of the above-mentioned act will have effect in relation to the field, stable, cow-shed, or other premises aforesaid].

Dated this —— day of ———, 18—.

(Signed)

A. B.

(3.)

Notice of declaration to adjoining occupiers.

[The contagious diseases (animals) act, 1869.]

To E. T., of ——— :

I, A. B., of ———, the inspector appointed by ———, being the local authority for the [county] of ———, hereby give you notice that I have made a declaration, a copy whereof is indorsed on this notice [*copy of declaration as filled up and signed to be indorsed*], and that in consequence thereof the field, stable, cow-shed, or other premises therein described, with all lands and buildings contiguous thereto in the same occupation, have become and are an infected place, and the same will continue to be an infected place until the determination and declaration relative thereto of the local authority, as provided for in section ——— of the above-mentioned act. And I hereby require you, as an occupier of lands and buildings adjoining to such infected places, part [or the whole] whereof lies within one mile of the boundaries of the infected place, to take notice that in consequence of the declaration aforesaid the rules of the said act with respect to infected places will, until such determination and declaration of the local authority as aforesaid, apply and have effect to and in respect of the land and buildings of which you are occupier as if the same were actually within the limits of the infected place.

Dated this ——— day of ———, 18—.

(Signed) A. B.

The ninth schedule refers to the local authorities, &c., in Scotland.

District of local authority.	Description of local authority of district set opposite name.	Local rate.*	Clerk of local authority.
Counties including any town or place which does not return or contribute to return a member to Parliament.	The persons appointed as provided in Part X of this act.	....	Clerk of supply.
Burghs which return or contribute to return a member to Parliament.	The magistrates and town council.	....	Town clerk.

* Rate appointed to be levied in Part X of this act.

Several amendments and modifications to the above law have been made since its enactment, among which the following has the most important bearing upon cattle exported from the United States :

IV.—OTHER FOREIGN COUNTRIES.

11. In relation to foreign animals other than those brought from the Channel Islands and the Isle of Man, if and as long as, from time to time, the privy council are satisfied, with respect to any foreign country, that the laws thereof relating to the importation and exportation of animals, and to the prevention of the introduction or spreading of disease, and the general sanitary condition of animals therein, are such as to afford reasonable security against the importation therefrom of diseased animals, then, from time to time, the privy council, by general or special order, shall allow, animals, or any specified kind of animals, brought from that country, to be landed, without being subject, under the provisions of this schedule, to slaughter or to quarantine, and may for that purpose alter or add to those provisions, as the case may require; but every such order shall forthwith, after the making thereof, if Parliament is then sitting, and if not, then forthwith after the next meeting of Parliament, be laid before both houses of Parliament.

C

www.ingramcontent.com/pod-product-compliance
Lightning Source LLC
Chambersburg PA
CBHW020309090426
42735CB00009B/1281